W9-BLC-169

Selected Studies from
PROVERBS

BIBLE STUDY GUIDE

From the Bible-teaching ministry of

Charles R. Swindoll

INSIGHT FOR LIVING

Charles R. Swindoll graduated in 1963 from Dallas Theological Seminary and has served in pastorates over thirty years, including more than twenty-two years at the First Evangelical Free Church of Fullerton, California. His sermon messages have been aired over radio since 1979 as the "Insight for Living" broadcast. In addition to his church and radio ministries, Chuck enjoys writing. As a best-selling author, he has written numerous books and booklets on a variety of subjects.

Based on the outlines and transcripts of Chuck's sermons, the study guide text is co-authored by Lee Hough, a graduate of the University of Texas at Arlington and Dallas Theological Seminary. He also wrote the Living Insights sections.

Editor in Chief:
Cynthia Swindoll

Coauthor of Text:
Lee Hough

Assistant Editor:
Wendy Peterson

Copy Editors:
Deborah Gibbs
Cheryl Gilmore
Glenda Schlahta

Designer:
Gary Lett

Publishing System Specialist:
Bob Haskins

Director, Communications Division:
Deedee Snyder

Manager, Creative Services:
Alene Cooper

Print Production Manager:
John Norton

Printer:
Sinclair Printing Company

Unless otherwise identified, all Scripture references are from the New American Standard Bible, © The Lockman Foundation 1960, 1962, 1963, 1968, 1971, 1972, 1973, 1975, 1977. Used by permission.

Scripture taken from the Holy Bible, New International Version, Copyright © 1973, 1978, 1984 International Bible Society, used by permission of Zondervan Bible Publishers [NIV].

Scripture taken from *The New Testament: A Private Translation in the Language of the People* by Charles B. Williams (Chicago, Ill.: Moody Press, 1958), [WILLIAMS].

The other translation cited is the Living Bible [LB].

Current guide coauthored by Lee Hough:
© 1994 Charles R. Swindoll. All rights reserved.
Outlines edited and expanded by Edgar Neuenschwander:
© 1983 Charles R. Swindoll. All rights reserved.
Original outlines published by Insight for Living:
© 1980 Charles R. Swindoll. All rights reserved.
Original outlines and transcripts:
© 1972, 1973, 1974, 1986 Charles R. Swindoll. All rights reserved.

An effort has been made to locate sources and obtain permission where necessary for the quotations used in this book. In the event of any unintentional omission, a modification will gladly be incorporated in future printings.

Notice
No portion of this publication may be translated into any language or reproduced in any form, except for brief quotations in reviews, without prior written permission of the publisher, Insight for Living, Post Office Box 69000, Anaheim, California 92817-0900.

ISBN 0-8499-8492-0
Printed in the United States of America
COVER DESIGN: Nina Paris
COVER PHOTOGRAPH: Jack Eadon Photographic
COVER GEMS: Courtesy of Lapidary International, Anaheim, California

CONTENTS

*These messages were not a part of the original series but are compatible with it.

INTRODUCTION

We often refer to the faith of Abraham, the patience of Job, and the courage of Elijah. As we turn to the ancient book of Proverbs, we come to the wisdom of Solomon.

I have never (and I mean *never*) opened my Bible to Proverbs without finding a "nugget" or principle or insight that gave me just what I needed at the moment. This book is not only wise, it is relevant and timely . . . constantly up to date. And my, how convicting!

As we undertake this very practical study of selected proverbs, my desire is that you will realize anew how aware God is of your circumstances. May you and I both gain a whole new perspective on life as a result of these days we spend together, drinking in the pure, clean, and wholesome water of the Word. May we be nourished in our walk with the Lord!

The wisdom of Solomon need not remain within the lines of Proverbs. May it soon be seen in your life and mine.

Chuck Swindoll

Chuck Swindoll

PUTTING TRUTH
INTO ACTION

K nowledge apart from application falls short of God's desire for His children. He wants us to apply what we learn so that we will change and grow. This study guide was prepared with these goals in mind. As you go through the following pages, we hope your desire to discover biblical truth will grow as your understanding of God's Word increases and that you will be encouraged to apply what you've learned.

To assist you in your study, we've included a section called ⚡ **Living Insights** at the end of each lesson. These exercises will challenge you to study further and to think of specific ways to put your discoveries into action.

There are many ways to use this guide—in personal devotions, group studies, discussions with friends and family, and Sunday school classes. And, of course, it's an ideal study aid when you're listening to its corresponding "Insight for Living" radio series.

To benefit most from this study guide, we would encourage you to consider it a spiritual journal. That's why we've included space in the **Living Insights** for recording your thoughts and discoveries. We hope you'll return to those sections often for review and encouragement as you continue to grow in your walk with Christ.

Lee M. Hough

Lee Hough
Coauthor of Text
Author of Living Insights

Selected Studies from
PROVERBS

Chapter 1

VERTICAL WISDOM FOR HORIZONTAL LIVING

Proverbs 1:1–9

Since 1955 knowledge has doubled every five years; libraries groan with the weight of new books. . . . In fact, our generation possesses more data about the universe and human personality than all previous generations put together. High school graduates to-day have been exposed to more information about the world than Plato, Aristotle, Spinoza or Benjamin Franklin. In terms of facts alone, neither Moses nor Paul could pass a college entrance exam today.

Yet by everyone's standards, even with all our knowledge . . . society today is peopled with a bumper crop of brilliant failures. . . . Men and women educated to earn a living often don't know anything about handling life itself. Alumni from noted universities have mastered information about a narrow slice of life but couldn't make it out of the first grade when it comes to living successfully with family and friends. Let's face it. Knowledge is not enough to meet life's problems. We need wisdom, the ability to handle life with skill.[1]

Where can we find this rare, intangible quality—and how? By mining the mother lode of practical insights divinely deposited in the book of Proverbs. Unlike the Psalms, which deepen

---

1. Hadden Robinson, from the foreword to Robert L. Alden's *Proverbs: A Commentary on an Ancient Book of Timeless Advice* (Grand Rapids, Mich.: Baker Book House, 1983), p. 7.

our devotional life with God, Proverbs enriches our ability to cope with daily life and other people.

Do you need wisdom so you can become skilled at godly living? Then stake your claim in Proverbs, one of the richest veins of vertical wisdom for horizontal living ever discovered.

To begin, let's conduct a general survey of the book's origin and purposes. Then, in subsequent chapters, we'll focus our energies on excavating nuggets of wisdom related to difficult areas of practical living.

The Name of the Book

Clearly visible on the surface of verse 1 are the name and author of the book: "The proverbs of Solomon the son of David, king of Israel." Commentator Robert Alden writes, "Just as we associate the law with Moses and David with the Psalms, so we put wisdom and Solomon together."[2] Solomon, however, did not compose the entire book. Chapter 30, for example, was penned by an individual named Agur (v. 1), and the insights of chapter 31 were taught to King Lemuel by his mother (v. 1).

The name Proverbs comes from the Hebrew root word *mashal*, meaning "to represent, be like." It connotes making a comparison to convey a specific truth in a pointed way. The book is filled with sayings, many brief, to guide the life of the godly. One person defined these pithy sayings as "short sentences drawn from long experience."

The Contents of the Book

The capsules of truth presented in Proverbs come mostly in one of three kinds of couplets. Some are *contrastive*, using the word *but*, as in 13:1:

A wise son accepts his father's discipline,
But a scoffer does not listen to rebuke.
(see also vv. 10, 18, 24)

Others are *completive*, using the words *and* or *so*, as in 14:10:

The heart knows its own bitterness,
And a stranger does not share its joy.
(see also v. 13; 16:3)

2. Alden, *Proverbs*, p. 19.

And still others are *comparative*, using the words *better/than* or *like/so*, as in 15:16–17:

> Better is a little with the fear of the Lord,
> Than great treasure and turmoil with it.
> Better is a dish of vegetables where love is,
> Than a fattened ox and hatred with it.
> (see also 25:24–25)

In addition to using couplets to impart truth, Solomon also relies on the cameo appearances of a wide cast of characters.[3] Together, the couplets and characters help prepare us to deal wisely with life's knotty issues. As psychologist Jay Adams points out, there are basically four ways of dealing with problems: we can avoid them; we can allow them to deflect us from our goals; we can view our situation as hopeless and simply give up; or we can work through the issue to a healthy resolution.[4]

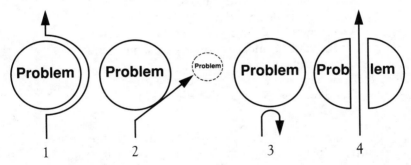

Proverbs is filled with direct, practical counsel that enables its readers to choose option four illustrated above. For example, to deal with the problem of lust, Solomon advises:

> Reproofs for discipline are the way of life,
> To keep you from the evil woman,
> From the smooth tongue of the adulteress.
> Do not desire her beauty in your heart,
> Nor let her catch you with her eyelids. (6:23b–25)

3. From a personal study on counseling in Proverbs, Chuck once counted forty-six specific kinds of men, twenty-three kinds of women, and several types of children.

4. See Jay E. Adams, *Competent to Counsel* (Phillipsburg, N.J.: Presbyterian and Reformed Publishing Co., 1970), pp. 129–30.

The context is that of a father speaking to his son, and his words cut right through to a solution: To resist lust's temptations, you must guard your heart. In other words, do not meditate on impure thoughts. Do not cultivate base imaginations. Don't linger with lustful eyes. Solomon doesn't engage in wishful thinking or abstract theorizing; he gives inspired, straightforward help.

The Purposes of the Book

Now let's dig a little deeper into chapter 1 and uncover the five specific purposes of Proverbs.

> To know wisdom and instruction,
> To discern the sayings of understanding,
> To receive instruction in wise behavior,
> Righteousness, justice and equity;
> To give prudence to the naive,
> To the youth knowledge and discretion,
> A wise man will hear and increase in learning,
> And a man of understanding will acquire wise
>   counsel,
> To understand a proverb and a figure,
> The words of the wise and their riddles.
> (vv. 2–6)

First: *To revere and obey God from the heart.* Solomon reveals his first purpose in verse 2a, "to know wisdom and instruction." The term *wisdom* is key to this book, so let's examine its meaning with the help of commentator Sid Buzzell.

> Of the several words for wisdom and related synonyms used in Proverbs, the primary and most frequent one is *hokmâh*. It occurs 45 times in Proverbs. In the Old Testament *hokmâh* is used of the skill of craftsmen, sailors, singers, mourners, administrators, and counselors. These workers and others, being knowledgeable, experienced, and efficient in their areas of expertise, were considered skillful; they were therefore "wise." Similarly in the spiritual realm a person who possesses *hokmâh* in reference to God is one who is both knowledgeable and experienced in following God's way. So in the Bible's Wisdom

4

literature being wise means being skilled in godly living. Having God's wisdom means having the ability to cope with life in a God-honoring way.[5]

Closely connected to wisdom is our need for "instruction." More than just the communication of facts, the term Solomon uses for this word means "discipline, chastening, or correction." The person who is wise in godly living exercises moral discipline. As commentator Derek Kidner points out, "Wisdom will be hard-won, a quality of character as much as of mind."[6]

Second: *To provide discernment to the eye.* This next purpose comes from the second half of verse 2, "To discern the sayings of understanding." *Discern* means "understand, consider, perceive."[7] It's the ability to read between the lines, to distinguish truth from error, right from wrong, good from evil (see 1 Kings 3:9). The *Theological Wordbook of the Old Testament* adds that it is "a power of judgment and perceptive insight and is demonstrated in the use of knowledge."[8] A little later in this same source we're also told that from a number of instances,

> insight or moral understanding is a gift from God (Dan 2:21) and is not the fruit of empiricism. It is ethical discernment. A person prays for it (Ps 119:34) and since this insight is uniquely God's, he can reveal or conceal it (Isa 29:14). . . .
>
> While understanding it is a gift of God, it does not come automatically. The possession of it requires a persistent diligence. It is more than IQ; it connotes character. One is at fault if he doesn't have it and in fact, not to pursue it will incur God's punishment (Prov 2:1f; Ruth 1:21f).[9]

5. Sid S. Buzzell, "Proverbs," in *The Bible Knowledge Commentary*, Old Testament ed., ed. John F. Walvoord and Roy B. Zuck (Wheaton, Ill.: Scripture Press Publications, Victor Books, 1985), p. 902.

6. Derek Kidner, *The Proverbs: An Introduction and Commentary* (Downers Grove, Ill.: InterVarsity Press, 1964), p. 36.

7. R. Laird Harris, Gleason L. Archer, Jr., and Bruce K. Waltke, eds., *Theological Wordbook of the Old Testament* (Chicago, Ill.: Moody Press, 1980), vol. 1, p. 103.

8. Harris, Archer, and Waltke, *Theological Wordbook*, vol. 1, p. 103.

9. Harris, Archer, and Waltke, *Theological Wordbook*, vol. 1, pp. 103–4.

Third: *To develop alertness in the walk.* We are, according to Proverbs 1:3,

> To receive instruction in wise behavior,
> Righteousness, justice, and equity.

The word *receive* "suggests action or mobility. It's the term associated with 'plucking grapes and taking them with you.' In this instance, it refers to instruction that is to be plucked and taken like succulent fruit from a vine."[10]

Fourth: *To establish discretion and purpose in life.* This objective is somewhat different from the others because we're told in verse 4 the kind of persons Proverbs will benefit most.

> To give prudence to the naive.
> To the youth knowledge and discretion.

In its root form, the Hebrew term for *naive* means to "be open, spacious, wide."[11] The simple person is wide open, easily influenced, gullible; an easy target for someone such as the harlot described in chapter 7. As for the "youth" Solomon mentions, this refers to anyone between birth and marriageable age—small children, early adolescent teens, young adults.

What will Proverbs do for the simple and the young? (1) The naive will become prudent, which *Webster's* defines as being "shrewd in the management of practical affairs."[12] Prudent individuals demonstrate good common sense. And (2) for the young who practice the wisdom of Proverbs, the reward is "discretion." C. H. Toy defines this as "the power of forming plans."[13] Derek Kidner adds,

> The godly man is in the best sense a man of affairs, who takes the trouble to know his way about, and plan his course realistically (*cf.* 22:3: "a shrewd man sees danger and hides himself; but the simple go on, and suffer for it").[14]

---

10. From the study guide *You and Your Problems*, coauthored by Lee Hough, from the Bible-teaching ministry of Charles R. Swindoll (Fullerton, Calif.: Insight for Living, 1989), p. 3.

11. R. Laird Harris, Gleason L. Archer, Jr., and Bruce K. Waltke, eds., *Theological Wordbook of the Old Testament* (Chicago, Ill.: Moody Press, 1980), vol. 2, p. 742.

12. *Merriam-Webster's Collegiate Dictionary*, 10th ed., see "prudent."

13. C. H. Toy, as quoted by Kidner in *Proverbs*, p. 37.

14. Kidner, *Proverbs*, p. 37.

Fifth: *To cultivate a keenness of mind.* This last purpose is found in 1:6.

> To understand a proverb and a figure,
> The words of the wise and their riddles.

According to Buzzell, "the word for 'riddle' (*hîdâh*) means an indirect, oblique, or enigmatic statement (like a figure of speech) which needs interpretation."[15] An in-depth study of Proverbs will "introduce the reader to a style of teaching that provokes his thought, getting under his skin by thrusts of wit, paradox, common sense and teasing symbolism."[16] Exercising our minds in such a variety of ways will inevitably sharpen our ability to think deeply, as the psalmist affirms:

> O how I love Thy law!
> It is my meditation all the day.
> Thy commandments make me wiser than my enemies,
> For they are ever mine.
> I have more insight than all my teachers,
> For Thy testimonies are my meditation.
> I understand more than the aged,
> Because I have observed Thy precepts.
> (Ps. 119:97–100)

The Goal of the Book

In closing, notice three key sources of wisdom mentioned in Proverbs 1:7–9.

> The fear of the Lord is the beginning of knowledge;
> Fools despise wisdom and instruction.
> Hear, my son, your father's instruction,
> And do not forsake your mother's teaching;
> Indeed, they are a graceful wreath to your head,
> And ornaments about your neck.

The fear of the Lord, a father's instruction, and a mother's teaching—all three impart wisdom. And wisdom is not a burdensome load that will weigh down your life but a treasure that will add grace and beauty to your days.

15. Buzzell, "Proverbs," p. 907.
16. Kidner, *Proverbs*, pp. 58–59.

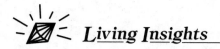

To begin prospecting for the wealth of wisdom in Proverbs, dig in with your mental spade right now and memorize Proverbs 1:7.

> The fear of the Lord is the beginning of knowledge;
> Fools despise wisdom and instruction.

Next, listen to LeRoy Eims as he explains the rich meaning behind the concept of fearing God.

> What does this expression mean? Some say it means reverential trust, or affectionate reverence. . . .
>
> Let us not forget, however, that when God gave His law to His people, He did so to the accompaniment of thunder and lightning and thick smoke. The people at the foot of Mount Sinai trembled. When we think of the fear of the Lord, let us not eliminate altogether the plain old "being afraid of God." Remember the words of the New Testament, "It is a fearful thing to fall into the hands of the living God" (Heb. 10:31).
>
> The first result of this godly fear is that God must be reverenced for who He is. . . .
>
> Second, God is to be served. If He is truly Almighty God, if we are His people, if we are living in His Word through a daily experience with Him, it behooves each one of us to find our place of service to Him and joyfully give our lives to the responsibility God has placed before us.
>
> Third, God is to be worshiped. Jesus, in His encounter with the woman at the well of Sychar in Samaria, told her, "But the hour cometh, and now is, when the true worshipers shall worship the Father in spirit and in truth, for the Father seeketh such to worship Him. God is a Spirit, and they that worship Him must worship Him in spirit and in truth" (John 4:23–24).
>
> Fourth, God is to be obeyed. Solomon also wrote, "Let us hear the conclusion of the whole matter: fear God, and keep His commandments, for this is the

whole duty of man. For God shall bring every work into judgment, with every secret thing, whether it be good, or whether it be evil" (Eccles. 12:13–14).

Because of all that God has done for us in His grace and mercy, showered on us in Jesus Christ, we are to love Him with all our hearts, souls, and minds. The Apostle John taught, "We love Him because He first loved us" (1 John 4:19). So when you add it all up, that we should reverence God, serve Him, worship Him, obey Him, and love Him, that is a picture of the beginning of knowledge. And only fools despise it.[17]

Do you "fear the Lord"? In this next Living Insight, let's do a little panning for this precious attitude in the daily flow of our own lives.

Living Insights

STUDY TWO

Pause for a moment to sift through this past week and identify the practical ways in which you reverenced the Lord. If you need help knowing what to look for, reread the five results of fearing God that LeRoy Eims noted in the first Living Insight.

_____

_____

_____

_____

_____

What are some of the ways you've seen other believers demonstrate a fear of the Lord?

_____

_____

_____

17. LeRoy Eims, *Wisdom from Above* (Wheaton, Ill.: Scripture Press Publications, Victor Books, 1978), pp. 17–18.

Is there something you want to imitate or adapt to strengthen your fear of the Lord?

_____

_____

_____

———————◆———————

To enrich your exploration of Proverbs, read one chapter a day for the next thirty-one days—starting today!

Chapter 2

WARNINGS AGAINST
REFUSING REPROOF

Proverbs 1:20–33

We began our study of Proverbs in the last chapter "by breaking up the plain daylight of wisdom (*hokmá*) into its rainbow of constituent colours."[1] Instruction, discernment, prudence—these are but a few of the many shades of wisdom we examined closely.

Now let's familiarize ourselves with wisdom from a completely different perspective. Beginning in verse 20 of chapter 1, Solomon presents wisdom to us as a person. No longer just an abstract principle to be dissected with definitions, wisdom now speaks to us personified as a woman.

Some Basic Facts about Wisdom

Allow us to acquaint you with certain facts about "Lady Wisdom."

First: Wisdom Is Available

Wisdom shouts in the street,
She lifts her voice in the square;
At the head of the noisy streets she cries out;
At the entrance of the gates in the city, she
    utters her sayings. (vv. 20–21)

Wisdom is not shy. As you can see, she's very accessible and easy to find. In fact, she goes out of her way to speak to us through God's Word, creation, and the lessons of daily life.

Second: Wisdom Can Be Ignored and Spurned

"I called, and you refused;
I stretched out my hand, and no one paid attention;
And you neglected all my counsel,
And did not want my reproof." (vv. 24–25)

Our problem is not exposure to wisdom—our problem is putting

---

1. Derek Kidner, *The Proverbs: An Introduction and Commentary* (Downers Grove, Ill.: Inter-Varsity Press, 1964), p. 36.

her words into practice. So often we stroll by wisdom's outstretched hand, tossing a careless "No, thank you" over our shoulders as we crane our necks to find someone with more pleasing ideas (see 2 Tim. 4:2–4). Proverbs 1:22 names three types of individuals who consistently shun wisdom.

> "How long, O naive ones, will you love simplicity?
> And scoffers delight themselves in scoffing,
> And fools hate knowledge?"

The naive. As you may recall from the first lesson, the naive or simple individual lacks discernment. He or she is easily enchanted by the music of pied pipers, blindly following them wherever they lead.

The scoffer. This is the skeptic, the mocker, someone who contemptuously disagrees with anything that opposes his or her own ideas.

The fool. Typically, when we think of a fool, we picture someone who lacks intelligence. But the biblical meaning of *fool* is "not so much one lacking in mental powers, as one who misuses them; not one who does not reason, but reasons wrongly."[2]

Third: Wisdom Spurned Bears Serious Consequences

> "Because I called and you refused; . . .
> I will even laugh at your calamity;
> I will mock when your dread comes,
> When your dread comes like a storm,
> And your calamity comes on like a whirlwind,
> When distress and anguish come on you.
> Then they will call on me, but I will not answer;
> They will seek me diligently, but they shall not
>   find me, . . .
> So they shall eat of the fruit of their own way,
> And be satiated with their own devices.
> For the waywardness of the naive shall kill them,
> And the complacency of fools shall destroy
>   them." (vv. 24a, 26–28, 31–32)

When we've rejected wisdom's healthy counsel month after month, year after year, and sated ourselves instead on the world's artificially sweetened advice, we can expect some heartburn. But God doesn't offer any panic packages of wisdom that can plop-plop-

---

2. Merrill F. Unger, *Unger's Bible Dictionary*, 3d ed. (Chicago, Ill.: Moody Press, 1966), p. 375.

fizz-fizz our problems away. It'll take a careful new diet and strenuous exercise to shape up those sour situations and distorted values.[3] How much better to heed wisdom's counsel from the beginning and reap the rewards promised in verse 33:

> "But he who listens to me shall live securely,
> And shall be at ease from the dread of evil."

The Connection between Wisdom and Reproof

Let's shift our attention away from Lady Wisdom herself now and focus instead on how she comes to us. What avenue does God frequently use to get our attention so that we'll heed her voice? See if you can pick out the answer that's repeated in these three verses.

> "Turn to my reproof,
> Behold, I will pour out my spirit on you;
> I will make my words known to you. . . .
> And you neglected all my counsel,
> And did not want my reproof; . . .
> They would not accept my counsel,
> They spurned all my reproof." (vv. 23, 25, 30)

If you guessed "reproof," you're right. Wisdom comes to us when we accept and adjust to God's reproofs, that is to say, His reprimands, cautions, and counsel. Commentator Robert Alden notes,

> Criticism is hard to take; few respond to it with ease. It is ego-damaging, yet accepting it and changing in response to it is the only way to succeed. Soil must be plowed, harrowed, and broken before it can be used. Clay must be kneaded and pounded before it can be shaped into a useful or beautiful vessel. People too must sometimes be broken in order to have bad habits and attitudes replaced with good ones. Blessed are those who take this sage's advice and listen to criticism.[4]

---

3. Adapted from the study guide *You and Your Problems*, coauthored by Lee Hough, from the Bible-teaching ministry of Charles R. Swindoll (Fullerton, Calif.: Insight for Living, 1989), p. 4–5.

4. Robert L. Alden, *Proverbs: A Commentary on an Ancient Book of Timeless Advice* (Grand Rapids, Mich.: Baker Book House, 1983), p. 28.

Sometimes God's reproofs come to us *directly* through His Word:

> "For the commandment is a lamp, and the teach-
> ing is a light;
> And reproofs for discipline are the way of life."
> (Prov. 6:23; see also Ps. 119:33–40 and
> 2 Tim. 3:16–17).

The Lord also uses *indirect* means to correct us, such as life's experiences or other people. For example, when your child says, "Dad, aren't you supposed to stop on red?" Or when everyone else arrives at the meeting on time except you. Or when you're driving home after overeating at a restaurant and you pass someone jogging beside the road.

What qualities are these direct and indirect reproofs designed to develop in us? Here are just a few for you to ponder.

Alertness	Discernment	Love	Sincerity
Appreciation	Discipline	Loyalty	Submissiveness
Compassion	Efficiency	Objectivity	Tactfulness
Confidentiality	Enthusiasm	Patience	Teachability
Consistency	Flexibility	Peacefulness	Thoroughness
Cooperativeness	Gentleness	Punctuality	Thoughtfulness
Courtesy	Honesty	Self-control	Tolerance
Creativity	Humility	Sense of Humor	Understanding
Dependability	Initiative	Sensitivity	Unselfishness

Don't let this list overwhelm you; instead, let it be an inspiration!

Why Reproof Is Refused

Unfortunately, Christians who humbly accept reproof are rare. Why? At least four reasons can be gleaned on a closer inspection of verses 24–25 in Proverbs 1.

1. *Willful refusal:* "Because I called, and you refused" (v. 24a). Wisdom is speaking—she entreats you and me to receive her counsel, but often we deliberately ignore her. Not because we fail to hear her or misunderstand her words; rather, it's because we're sinful and self-centered and hate to bow the knee to anyone's authority except our own.

For an even clearer picture of just how stubborn this kind of rejection is, consider this: the same word for *refused* used here is also used of Pharaoh when he refused to let Israel go despite God's repeated reproofs (see Exod. 4:23; 7:14; 10:3).

2. *Insensitivity:* "I stretched out my hand, and no one paid attention" (Prov. 1:24b). To be insensitive means to lack awareness or alertness. It corresponds with the New Testament phrase, "dull of hearing" (Heb. 5:11; compare Matt. 13:15). Reproofs come, but we're not even aware of them. We're not sensitive to God's correction through His Word or other people. Why? Oftentimes it's because we're so preoccupied with life. Financial pressures, work woes, and relational rifts overwhelm us, and we become like horses wearing blinders, seeing only the problems straight in front of us. Then, too, there's sometimes the problem of overexposure to church. After years of sitting in the same pew, the truths of Scripture are so familiar to some of us that our hearts have stopped really hearing them.

3. *Indifference:* "And you neglected all my counsel" (Prov. 1:25a). The indifferent person says, "Point out all the wrong about me you like, I just don't care." People who respond in this manner are often depressed. Look, for example, at 15:32, where the same term for *neglects* is used and notice how the indifferent individual is described:

> He who neglects discipline despises himself,
> But he who listens to reproof acquires understanding.

Depression can induce people to despise themselves so deeply that they carelessly shrug their shoulders at reproof because nothing really seems to matter anymore—or else things seem so bad that they've decided to just give up.

4. *Defensiveness:* "And did not want my reproof" (1:25b). Instead of admitting wrong, some people vigorously defend their deficiencies. You've heard the excuses before— "But you don't understand!" or, "I don't deserve this!" or, "I can't help it, it's just the way I am." No matter how clearly wrong these individuals are, they simply won't admit fault. In their minds it's always the other person who should change.

Willful refusal, insensitivity, indifference, defensiveness—are any of these an uncomfortable reminder of the way you reacted to a recent reproof? Perhaps the correction came from a parent, a pastor, a teacher, or even a letter from a friend. We all know how painful those times can be. But just remember, only those sensitive and responsive to Lady Wisdom enjoy the reward of skillful godly living.

May these words from the writer of Hebrews encourage you to embrace wisdom the next time she calls.

All discipline for the moment seems not to be joyful,
but sorrowful; yet to those who have been trained
by it, afterwards it yields the peaceful fruit of
righteousness. (Heb. 12:11)

 **_Living Insights_**

It's a wise man who profits by his own experience,
but it's a good deal wiser one who lets the rattlesnake
bite the other fellow.[5]

Let's examine the snakebites of others who ignored wisdom's
reproofs and walked right into a viper's den of painful consequences.
We've already mentioned Pharaoh as an example of willful refusal.
Can you think of another, not only for this category but also for
the other three? In case you need help, here are a few passages to
get you started: Genesis 4:1–9; 1 Samuel 3:11–18; 15:1–28; Matthew 19:16–24; 23:13–37.

Willful refusal: _____

_____

_____

_____

Insensitivity: _____

_____

_____

_____

Indifference: _____

_____

_____

5. Henry Wheeler Shaw, as quoted in *The International Dictionary of Thoughts*, comp. John P.
Bradley, Leo F. Daniels, and Thomas C. Jones (Chicago, Ill.: J. G. Ferguson Publishing Co.,
1969), p. 774.

16

Defensiveness: _____

_____

_____

_____

☼ *Living Insights*

No matter how we refuse reproof, whether willfully, indifferently, or in some other way, the reason for it is usually the same—self-protection. None of us likes admitting to faults, because our sense of self-worth is directly tied to our performance. Wisdom's reproofs threaten our ego.

But what if . . . what if we changed our basic goal in life? What if, instead of protecting ourselves, we committed ourselves to becoming like Christ? How would we respond to wisdom then? Defensively? Indifferently? Not hardly. When conformity to Christ becomes our deep-seated desire, we welcome reproof. Sure, it's still painful at times, but that's because our old self hates being passed over in favor of the new self being created in the image of Christ (see Col. 3:9–10).

Tell me what you know about self-protection. How does it manifest itself in your responses to reproof?

_____

_____

_____

_____

_____

_____

Based on the way you typically respond to reproof, what would you say is your goal? Self-protection or Christlikeness?

17

Chapter 3

FOR MINERS ONLY

Proverbs 2:1–9

As we work our way deeper into the mine shaft of Proverbs, we come to a sign posted above the entrance of chapter 2 that reads: FOR MINERS ONLY. It's the end of the line for the tourist and the timid. Only those willing to wear the hard hat of commitment are encouraged to go beyond this point. From now on the digging becomes more personal and intense.

Are you still eager to excavate? Then let's enter chapter 2, where we'll be given four tools and the training to use them to extract King Solomon's treasures.

The Conditions

The first tool handed to us is in the couplet of verse 1.

Discipline of the Written Word

> My son, . . . receive my sayings,
> And treasure my commandments within you.

The "sayings" and "commandments" are God's Word, and to wield it correctly in our mining efforts we must do two things.

First, *possess the right attitude toward God's Word.* Our attitude toward the Bible determines virtually everything about how skillfully we live the Christian life. If we're receptive, eager to take the Scriptures into our hands, our reward will be great. But if we flippantly ignore it, we'll be no more successful at finding His riches than if we tried to pry precious gems from rocks with our bare hands.

Second, *saturate your mind with God's Word.* Long ago the prophet Hosea lamented, "My people are destroyed for lack of knowledge" (4:6). The Israelites neglected to store up the Law in their hearts, and they starved spiritually. The right handling of God's Word includes hearing, reading, studying, memorizing, and meditating on it. Such diligent cultivation will result in a rich harvest of wisdom—and that is one treasure the Lord wants us to hoard (see also Ps. 119:11).

Discipline of Inner Desire

Moving on to the next couplet, we find our second tool.

> Make your ear attentive to wisdom,
> Incline your heart to understanding. (Prov. 2:2)

Lose this tool, this longing for God's wisdom, and we face the peril A. W. Tozer wrote of in his book *The Divine Conquest*.

> Is it not true that for most of us who call ourselves Christians there is no real experience? We have substituted theological ideas for an arresting encounter; we are full of religious notions, but our great weakness is that for our hearts there is no one there.
>
> Whatever else it embraces, true Christian experience must always include a genuine encounter with God. Without this, religion is but a shadow, a reflection of reality, a cheap copy of an original once enjoyed by someone else of whom we have heard.[1]

What must we do to dig for wisdom with the right motivation, rather than only go through the motions of mining and end up empty-handed?

First, *have an attentive ear*. Have you ever been near a mom in a bustling home when she suddenly says, "Excuse me, my baby's crying, I need to go check on her," but all you hear is the babel of people talking? Isn't it amazing how sensitively tuned a parent's ear can be to a child's voice? We can develop that same keen receptivity toward our heavenly Father by honing a sensitive ear to His reproofs. Ask God to make you attentive to wisdom's voice.

Second, *cultivate an open heart*. With the ear we receive wisdom and with the heart we store it up. But not just any heart can hold this particular kind of treasure. Only one that is *inclined*—stretched out, opened up—has such a capacity.

Discipline of Prevailing Prayer

The third tool to become familiar with is found in the couplet of verse 3.

> . . . Cry for discernment,
> Lift your voice for understanding.

Perhaps the most difficult mining tool to master is consistent, fervent prayer. It's said that Martin Luther set apart the three best

1. A. W. Tozer, *The Divine Conquest* (Camp Hill, Pa.: Christian Publications, 1978), p. 26.

hours of his day to pray. Most of us, however, can't imagine spending thirty minutes even on our best day. What can we do to improve?

First, *proclaim the need for discernment.* How many of us have wasted our time wishing for discernment instead of actually asking God for it through prayer? "You do not have because you do not ask," James pointedly reminds us (James 4:2b). And the same is also true concerning Solomon's second exhortation.

Second, *request understanding.* James has also said that "if any of you lacks wisdom, let him ask of God, who gives to all men generously and without reproach, and it will be given to him" (1:5). Who do we ask? Where do we look for wisdom? God! He is the source we must earnestly beseech for the wisdom we need (read Job 28:1, 12–15, 20–21, 23–24, 28). Can we honestly say that we do?

Discipline of Daily Consistency

Finally, the couplet in Proverbs 2:4 brings us our last tool.

. . . Seek her as silver,
And search for her as for hidden treasures.

All of us have our hot and cold moments spiritually, but to become successful miners of God's wisdom we must have some measure of consistency about our daily digging. For that to happen, remember these two tips.

First, *seek wisdom with diligence,* and second, *pursue it with patience.* The Hebrew term for *seek* doesn't connote a glance here or there. It's the idea of a person relentlessly searching for something with the full expectation of finding it.[2] Mining is demanding work. The precious stones of discernment and understanding are "not usually discovered by a casual observer or chance passerby. They are excavated and enjoyed instead by the diligent, devoted, and determined."[3]

The Results

What happens *if* we receive Solomon's sayings (v. 1), and *if* we cry to God for discernment (v. 3), and *if* we seek understanding as

2. R. Laird Harris, Gleason L. Archer, Jr., and Bruce K. Waltke, eds., *Theological Wordbook of the Old Testament* (Chicago, Ill.: Moody Press, 1980), vol. 1, p. 129.

3. Robert L. Alden, *Proverbs: A Commentary on an Ancient Book of Timeless Advice* (Grand Rapids, Mich.: Baker Book House, 1983), p. 32.

silver (v. 4)? Verse 5 announces our reward:

> Then you will discern the fear of the Lord,
> And discover the knowledge of God.

The prize we seek is twofold. "The fear of the Lord"—a deep, awesome respect, and "the knowledge of God"—a bosom nearness to Him. Derek Kidner wonderfully describes these as "the poles of awe and intimacy."[4] Read carefully Tozer's explanation of how saints throughout time have experienced these two rewards.

> The spiritual giants of old were [those] who at some time became acutely conscious of the real Presence of God and maintained that consciousness for the rest of their lives. The first encounter may have been one of terror, as when a "horror of great darkness" fell upon Abram, or as when Moses at the bush hid his face because he was afraid to look upon God. Usually this fear soon lost its content of terror and changed after a while to delightsome awe, to level off finally into a reverent sense of complete nearness to God.[5]

The Promises

Mining has always been a risky endeavor. The lure of fabulous riches has left many a prospector penniless. So what surety do we have that, if we dig as Solomon has directed, we will discover the rich rewards promised in verse 5? Our guarantee is explained in verses 6–9:

> For the Lord gives wisdom;
> From His mouth come knowledge and understanding.
> He stores up sound wisdom for the upright;
> He is a shield to those who walk in integrity,
> Guarding the paths of justice,
> And He preserves the way of His godly ones.
> Then you will discern righteousness and justice
> And equity and every good course.

4. Derek Kidner, *The Proverbs: An Introduction and Commentary* (Downers Grove, Ill.: Inter-Varsity Press, 1964), p. 61.

5. Tozer, *The Divine Conquest*, pp. 26–27.

If we faithfully apply the mining tools and procedures outlined thus far, we can count on at least three benefits. First, *from within:* our hearts will be filled with wisdom, knowledge, and understanding (vv. 6–7a). Second, *from without:* God will provide protection (vv. 7b–8). This implies that we shall certainly encounter opposition, but the Lord promises to shield us, guard our path, and preserve our way. And third, *from above:* God will direct us into successful pursuits—righteousness, justice, equity, every good course—that give satisfaction (v. 9).

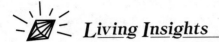 **Living Insights**

We've thrown a lot of training and equipment at you in this last lesson, so let's pause before we proceed any further for a little evaluation. Perhaps this will help you gain a realistic picture of the strengths and weaknesses of your own mining skills. Under each excavating technique, score the line at the point that best represents your level of ability.

I possess the right attitude toward God's Word.

Only on Sundays   Most Every Day

_____

I saturate my mind with God's Word.

Only on Sundays   Most Every Day

_____

I have an attentive ear.

Only on Sundays   Most Every Day

_____

I cultivate an open heart.

Only on Sundays   Most Every Day

_____

I proclaim the need for discernment.

Only on Sundays   Most Every Day

_____

I request understanding.

Only on Sundays   Most Every Day

_____

I seek wisdom with diligence.

Only on Sundays   Most Every Day

_____

I pursue wisdom with patience.

Only on Sundays   Most Every Day

_____

Living Insights

Now that you've finished the evaluation, write a brief summary outlining what you see as your strengths and weaknesses. Include an explanation as to why you think you're stronger in some areas than others. Finally, make a proposal detailing what you can begin doing this week to realistically improve your efforts at prospecting for the gold of God's wisdom.

Summary

_____

_____

_____

_____

_____

_____

_____

_____

_____

_____

_____

Proposal

_____

_____

_____

_____

_____

_____

_____

_____

Chapter 4

YOU AND YOUR HEART

Selected Proverbs

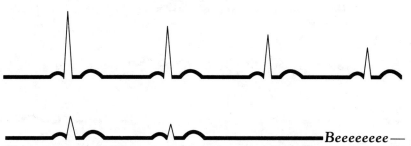

Beeeeeeee—
Emergency, Code Blue!—eeeeeeeeeeeeeee—Start chest compression.
Get the intubation ready. Someone bag first—eeeeeeee—Begin an epi
1 milligram IV push—eeeeeeee—no change; continue compression—
eeeeeeeee—Listen for breathing. Time? Four minutes—Let's shock
him, 300 watts—eeeeeeee—paddles ready. Everybody clear!
WHUMP—Rhythm check for pulse—eeeeeee—Still nothing. We're
losing him—eeeeeee—Another epi. Increase watts to 360—eeeeeee
eeeee—Charging . . .

It's hard to imagine that it could be you or me whose heart
stops like this one day. Most of the time we're not even aware of
the fist-sized muscle within our breasts that dutifully beats more
than one hundred thousand times a day. Nor are we conscious of
its powerful contractions that propel oxygen and nutrition through
more than sixty thousand miles of arteries, veins, and capillaries.
Yet when it hurts, we're in serious trouble. When it fails, we die.
And thousands are dying every day because of heart disease.

Even more epidemic, however, is the problem of spiritual heart
disease. You see, within each of us God has implanted another
"heart" we're often not aware of, whose beat reverberates in nearly
a thousand references in Scripture. Proverbs alone pulses with it
more than sixty-five times and in all but three of its chapters. Like
its physical counterpart, this intangible eternal organ is also suscep-
tible to disease. Sin has infected the heart of all Christians, causing

The section in this chapter entitled "What Does the Term *Heart* Mean?" has been adapted
from the study guide *A Ministry Everyone Would Respect*, coauthored by Ken Gire, from the Bible-
teaching ministry of Charles R. Swindoll (Fullerton, Calif.: Insight for Living, 1989), pp. 96–97.

all kinds of carnal coronary conditions. That's why Solomon warns,

> Watch over your heart with all diligence,
> For from it flow the springs of life. (Prov. 4:23)

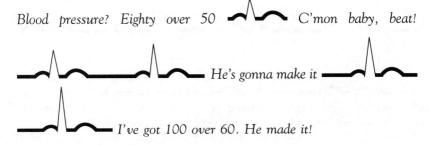

. . . All clear! WHUMP—eeeeeeeeee I'm getting a pulse.

Blood pressure? Eighty over 50 C'mon baby, beat!

He's gonna make it

I've got 100 over 60. He made it!

But will we—spiritually speaking? Just how healthy is your heart? Has sin blocked the flow of your prayers? Is your faith easily winded? Are you experiencing a numbing sensation in your conscience that makes it difficult to discern between good and evil? Many of us have similar symptoms. We're dangerously close to having a cardiac arrest.

Instead of waiting until we need 360 watts of scorching reproof to revive our hearts, why not stay healthy by practicing the type of preventive care Solomon prescribes in Proverbs? Interested? Then let's join him in the operating theater and conduct a thorough examination of the heart laid bare in Proverbs.

What Does the Term *Heart* Mean?

Biblically, the term *heart* represents our whole inner being. This is how the word is used in 1 Samuel 16:7:

> The Lord said to Samuel, "Do not look at his appearance or at the height of his stature, because I have rejected him; for God sees not as man sees, for man looks at the outward appearance, but the Lord looks at the heart."

In Proverbs, the Hebrew word predominantly used for *heart* is *leb*. It "not only includes the motives, feelings, affections, and desires, but also the will, the aims, the principles, the thoughts, and the intellect."[1]

The Greek word for *heart* is *kardia*, from which we form such words as *cardiology*. Gerhard Kittel, in his massive, nine-volume work on New Testament words, describes the term as follows:

> The heart is the centre of the inner life of man and the source or seat of all the forces and functions of soul and spirit. . . . Thus *[kardia]* comes to stand for the whole of the inner being of man in contrast to his external side. . . . The heart is supremely the one centre in man to which God turns, in which the religious life is rooted, which determines moral conduct.[2]

From Proverbs 2:2 to 31:11 Solomon repeatedly mentions the heart and, in doing so, provides us with a detailed picture of its inner workings. Let's look now at the wide variety of heart specimens he has on display.

Are There Various Kinds of Hearts?

Even a cursory glance of Proverbs reveals a broad diversity of hearts. For example:

A scheming heart (6:18a)	A righteous heart (15:28)
A cunning, sensual heart (7:9–10)	A glad heart (15:30)
A wise heart (10:8)	A haughty heart (18:12)
A deceptive heart (12:20)	A heart of rage (19:3)
A hurting heart (14:13)	A pure heart (22:11)
A tranquil heart (14:30)	An envious heart (23:17)

What is it that determines the kind of heart we will have? First of all, our *thoughts:* "For as he thinks within himself, so he is" (23:7a). We are what we think about. Someone once illustrated this beautifully, saying, "Sow a thought, reap an act. Sow an act, reap a habit. Sow a habit, reap your character. Sow your character, reap your destiny." It all begins with the seed thoughts we allow to flourish in our minds.

1. Robert Baker Girdlestone, *Synonyms of the Old Testament,* 2d ed. (1897; reprint, Grand Rapids, Mich.: William B. Eerdmans Publishing Co., n.d.), p. 65.

2. Gerhard Kittel, ed., *Theological Dictionary of the New Testament,* trans. Geoffrey W. Bromiley (Grand Rapids, Mich.: William B. Eerdmans Publishing Co., 1965), vol. 3, pp. 611–12.

A second major influence that molds the heart is our *speech*. "Death and life are in the power of the tongue" (18:21a). The tongue does more than just reveal what's in our hearts, it sparks other thoughts and consumes the thoughts of others around us. James warns, "Behold, how great a forest is set aflame by such a small fire! And the tongue . . . sets on fire the course of our life" (James 3:5b, 6b).

Third, our hearts are shaped by how we spend our *money*. "For where your treasure is, there will your heart be also" (Luke 12:34). What receives the greatest investment of your time and money? Your car, boat, home, hobby? Examine your checkbook. Read the expenditures like they were directions on a map and you'll likely find where your treasure is buried.

How about Specific Actions Prompted by the Heart?

Proverbs also reveals that the heart initiates certain bents or mindsets. Let's move the stethoscope of our attention around to four different passages and listen carefully for the specific action in each.

First: Spurns Reproof (5:12–13)

And you say, "How I have hated instruction!
And my heart spurned reproof!
And I have not listened to the voice of my teachers,
Nor inclined my ear to my instructors!"

Whoa! Watch your ears. The rebellious son pictured here fairly shouts as he recounts with agonizing self-reproach the many times he's refused wisdom. He has scoffed at his instructors, teachers, whomever wisdom put in his path. How many children have this same heart? How many aged? Solomon tells us in 10:8, "The wise of heart will receive commands." Humbly receive or pridefully reject—which response characterizes your heart?

Second: Bent on Sensuality (6:23–25a; 7:24–25a)

For the commandment is a lamp, and the teaching
      is light;
And reproofs for discipline are the way of life,
To keep you from the evil woman,
From the smooth tongue of the adulteress.
Do not desire her beauty *in your heart*. . . .
Now therefore, my sons, listen to me,

And pay attention to the words of my mouth.
Do not let your *heart* turn aside to her ways.
(emphasis added)

Notice that lust springs from a heart desire. And for various reasons, the heart of some individuals pumps nothing but the lurid and immoral into their imaginations. To cleanse the flow of our inner thoughts we must follow Solomon's practical advice. For example, be selective about what we allow our eyes to bring into our hearts (4:25–27); meditate on and obey wisdom's teachings (6:20–22); and don't resuscitate the sensual heart by dwelling on impure thoughts (v. 25a).

Third: Anxiety and Gloom (12:25a; 18:14)

Anxiety in the heart of a man weighs it down. . . .
The spirit of a man can endure his sickness,
But a broken spirit who can bear?

Anxiety anchors our spirits in a dark abyss of gloomy uncertainty and fear. Everything seems negative. Our laughter may take on a hollow ring: "Even in laughter the heart may be in pain, And the end of joy may be grief" (14:13). Only the heart unfettered with anxiety can experience the light buoyancy of joy.

A tranquil heart is life to the body. . . .
A joyful heart makes a cheerful face,
But when the heart is sad, the spirit is broken. . . .
All the days of the afflicted are bad,
But a cheerful heart has a continual feast.
(14:30a; 15:13, 15; see also 17:22)

Fourth: Indiscriminate Sharing (18:2)

A fool does not delight in understanding,
But only in revealing his own mind.

The verse literally says, "in revealing all of his *heart*" (emphasis added). Compare this to the verse in Judges 16, where Samson told Delilah "all that was in his heart" concerning the secret of his strength (v. 17). That indiscretion of indiscriminate sharing cost him his strength, his freedom, his eyes, and, ultimately, his life. Fools speak without thinking, and their careless babbling is their undoing. The wise, however, restrain words for their appropriate timing (see Prov. 12:23). They know when to cease talking and when to be transparent. "Like apples of gold in settings of silver," Solomon wrote, "Is a word spoken in right circumstances" (25:11).

Does God Give Us Any Practical Instruction for the Heart?

Today more than ever, people are concerned with eating right and exercising to maintain healthy hearts. We spend billions in a quest for fitness, all the while virtually ignoring the eternal heart that beats within the invisible realm of our spirit. Is it any wonder, then, why so many suffer from a weakened spiritual heart condition that makes it nearly impossible to fight the good fight, finish the course, or keep the faith (see 2 Tim. 4:7)?

As the personal physician for our true hearts, Solomon has already made one important recommendation that we noted at the beginning of this lesson—"Watch over your heart with all diligence, For from it flow the springs of life" (Prov. 4:23). Let's see what practical insights we can draw from these words to guide us in our pursuit of spiritual health.

Notice, first of all, that the verse opens with a command; not a wish, not a suggestion, but a direct order. Second, the reason we're ordered to guard our hearts carefully is explained in the latter half of the verse, "For from it flow the springs of life." Third, this command is given top priority, "with *all* diligence." We're to focus everything at our disposal to accomplish this objective. And, fourth, we're told that the outcome of our entire life depends on how well we obey this order.

The heart is where the Holy Spirit communicates truth. So guard that. Preserve that. "The springs of life" flow from within the holy ground of the heart, meaning God's direction and conviction. Nothing more sacred belongs to you than this vital organ. Keep watch over it well.

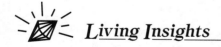 *Living* Insights

When was the last time you had your inner heart checked? Perhaps you're about due for a spiritual stress test to measure its overall health. To do this, we've provided you with several cardiograms to chart your heartbeat under varying conditions.

The first graph is a sample to help you see how it works. The main subject to be tested is finances. Now, we put the heart through

30

its paces in this area by indicating how strong or weak our spiritual pulse is under each of the related categories.

SAMPLE: **Finances**

| Give Generously | Give Regularly | Save Wisely | Live within My Means | Content with What I Have |

Home

| Put Others First | Patient with Spouse | Pray Regularly | Model Christ | Family Devotions |

Work

| Honest | Good Attitude | Servant to Others | Respect Authority | Work Is Above Standard | Initiate Ideas |

Friends

| Loyal | Truthful | Give Comfort in Conflict | Forgiving | Open | Encouraging |

Enemies

| Kind | Pray for Them | Refuse to Gossip | Ready to Forgive |

God

Bible Study   Prayer   Worship   Good Samaritan Lifestyle

_____

_____

_____

Once you've finished, write a summary of your findings in the space provided.

Test Results

_____

_____

_____

_____

_____

_____

_____

☀ *Living Insights*

As we mentioned in the lesson, Proverbs pulses with the beat of many different kinds of "hearts." To conduct a more in-depth study of their wide variety and their differences, look up in a concordance all the references to *heart* listed under Proverbs. As you read about each one, use the space provided to make observations, comparisons, or groupings. Also, in light of your test results from the first Living Insight, which heart from this study do you feel is most like your own?

Reference   Observations, Comparisons, and Groupings

_____   _____

_____   _____

_____   _____

_____   _____

_____   _____

_____   _____

_____   _____

_____   _____

_____   _____

_____   _____

_____   _____

_____   _____

_____   _____

_____   _____

_____   _____

_____   _____

_____   _____

_____   _____

_____   _____

_____   _____

_____   _____

The Heart(s) Most Like My Own

_____

_____

_____

_____

_____

_____

Chapter 5

YOU AND YOUR TONGUE

Selected Proverbs

The story is told of a woman who complained to a venerated Puritan minister about the clerical bands he wore with his pulpit gown. Saying that they annoyed her greatly because they were too long, she then asked his permission to shorten them. The aged saint quietly acquiesced and handed her the offending bands. Armed with her scissors, the woman shortened the bands according to her tastes and then handed the fragments back to the minister. Unruffled, he thanked her and said, "Now, my good woman, there is something about you that is altogether too long that has annoyed me greatly. And since one good turn deserves another, I would like permission to shorten it."

"Certainly," she said, "you have my permission and here are the scissors."

Whereupon the wise pastor said, "Very well, madam, put out your tongue."[1]

We've all known people, like that woman, whose tongues needed trimming. A boss, maybe, or a neighbor, or perhaps even an in-law. But if we're honest, we'll have to admit that our own tongues have probably needed paring a time or two as well. We've all done it— held someone up in a conversation like a paper doll and snipped away until nothing was left but pieces on the floor. Am I right?

Very well, then . . . put out your tongue. No, no, no. Relax, I'm not suggesting we shorten it with scissors. I just want to have a look at it. That's it, stick it out there. Hmmm, just as the apostle James said. OK, you can put that little beast back in its cage behind your teeth now. I'm afraid the diagnosis isn't good for either you or me. Listen to what the Holy Spirit inspired James to write about the tongue two millennia ago.

> The tongue is a small part of the body, and yet it
> boasts of great things. Behold, how great a forest is
> set aflame by such a small fire! And the tongue is a

---

1. Adapted from Clarence Edward Macartney, *Macartney's Illustrations* (New York, N.Y.: Abingdon-Cokesbury Press, 1950), p. 396.

fire, the very world of iniquity; the tongue is set among our members as that which defiles the entire body, and sets on fire the course of our life, and is set on fire by hell. For every species of beasts and birds, of reptiles and creatures of the sea, is tamed, and has been tamed by the human race. But no one can tame the tongue; it is a restless evil and full of deadly poison. (3:5–8)

As you can tell, James feels strongly about the tongue, and his bedside manner in describing it is pretty blunt. But are we really supposed to believe that the two-ounce muscle in our mouths is the problem? No. In Luke 6:45, Jesus unmasks the real culprit.

"The good man out of the good treasure of his heart
brings forth what is good; and the evil man out of
the evil treasure brings forth what is evil; for his
mouth speaks from that which fills his heart."

The tongue is actually neither friend nor foe. It's merely a messenger that delivers the dictates of the heart, either for good or evil. Wait . . . you may have read that last sentence too fast. Did you catch the part about the tongue being capable of *good* and not just evil? It's true. Solomon illustrated this important truth in Proverbs 15:2 by contrasting the words drawn from the wise and the foolish heart.

The tongue of the wise makes knowledge acceptable,
But the mouth of fools spouts folly.

For the rest of our time together in this lesson, let's consider four wise ways the tongue can be used for good. Then, in the next chapter, we'll examine some of the ways fools wag nothing but folly.

Right Uses of the Tongue

Using the tongue for good instead of evil is not something we all do automatically. We have to train ourselves by breaking bad habits and bridling our words to make them follow the paths of wise speech set forth in Proverbs. Let's travel down four of those paths for a closer look.

First: Wise Counsel, Sound Advice

The mouth of the righteous flows with wisdom. . . .
The lips of the wise spread knowledge. . . .

A wise man is he who listens to counsel.
(10:31a; 15:7a; 12:15b)

Life is full of difficult decisions that often leave us feeling over-whelmed, exasperated, and uncertain as to what we should do. "Lord, just tell me where to go to college, who to marry, what career to pursue, and where to live," we plead. But He doesn't typically make those decisions for us in some supernatural way. Rather, He helps us through the wise counsel of our godly friends and mentors. Even Solomon, gifted as he was, still understood his own need, and ours, for seeking counsel from others.

Oil and perfume make the heart glad,
So a man's counsel is sweet to his friend. . . .
Without consultation, plans are frustrated,
But with many counselors they succeed. (27:9; 15:22)

The next time a close friend has trouble clarifying the issues surrounding a crossroads decision, make your companion's heart glad with the sweet aroma of godly counsel.

Second: Reproof, Rebuke, Spiritual Exhortation

Another wise use of the tongue that's difficult for most to master is found in 27:6.

Faithful are the wounds of a friend,
But deceitful are the kisses of an enemy.
(see also 27:17)

The value of a reproof shared in genuine humility and compassion is impossible to measure. If you've ever experienced such an intimate exchange, you know that great insight and good are always gained. Why? Primarily because the one who wounds does so out of a deep love for the one being wounded. A true friend doesn't rush to rebuke another, wielding his or her words "rashly like the thrusts of a sword" (12:18a). People who delight in that kind of reckless reproof know nothing of love. Their tongues haven't been trained to bring healing, only hurt.

But the one who loves the other deeply rebukes reluctantly. He or she does not delight in confrontation. They anguish over the words that must be spoken. They pray with sweated brow for grace and humility. They're going to bruise the one they love, and such a duty is one of the most difficult and distasteful a friendship can bear. Yet even though the bruise may linger, the pain will subside and the two will draw closer. To bear the coveted title of best friend, we sometimes must go through the painful rite of reproof.

Third: Encouragement

A third way to honor the Lord with our lips is beautifully expressed in 16:24.

> Pleasant words are a honeycomb,
> Sweet to the soul and healing to the bones.

The seeming simplicity of encouragement sometimes fails to catch our attention. We tend to underestimate the power of this unfeigned tool of the tongue. Yet for those who have experienced the sweet taste of sincere affirmation, nothing could be more exhilarating. Near miracles are wrought because of it.

> A well-timed word has the power to urge a runner to finish the race, to rekindle hope when despair has set in, to spark a bit of warmth in an otherwise cold life, to trigger healthful self-evaluation in someone who doesn't think much about his shortcomings, to renew confidence when problems have the upper hand.[2]

All because of the unobtrusive but effective use of approving words. Is there someone who has impacted your life in this way—perhaps a parent, teacher, mentor, or loyal friend? Have you ever stopped to thank them with a letter or a phone call? Maybe this is your opportunity to encourage them.

But don't stop there. Think about the people who are around you on a regular basis. Your friends at work or in school. How about your spouse, a secretary, an associate, the gardener, or your children? Do you ever take the time to jot a note or meet with them privately to express how much you genuinely appreciate them and why? Think about it.

Fourth: Witnessing, Teaching, Comforting

> The tongue of the righteous is as choice silver. . . .
> The teaching of the wise is a fountain of life,

---

2. Lawrence J. Crabb, Jr. and Dan B. Allender, *Encouragement: The Key to Caring* (Grand Rapids, Mich.: Zondervan Publishing House, 1984), p. 25.

To turn aside from the snares of death.
(10:20a; 13:14)

When we are born again, we automatically become ambassadors for Christ (see 2 Cor. 5:20). Each of us bears the tremendous responsibility of communicating God's truth by our words as well as our deeds (see Matt. 5:16). That means the way we use our tongues can impact others for eternity. Solomon wrote, "Death and life are in the power of the tongue" (Prov. 18:21a), and that is an incredibly sobering thought. Don't let it restrain you from witnessing, teaching, or comforting. Rather, let it serve as a constant reminder and encouragement to engage in these kinds of ministries, for they are truly the right uses of the tongue.

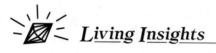 **Living Insights**   STUDY ONE

Many of us are familiar with the name Larry Crabb. He's the author of several outstanding works in the field of counseling, such as *Basic Principles of Biblical Counseling, Effective Biblical Counseling,* and *Inside Out.* He's also written many other well-known books, like *The Marriage Builder* and *Finding God.* He holds a Ph.D. in clinical psychology from the University of Illinois and is the founder and director of the Institute of Biblical Counseling in Morrison, Colorado. In addition to being a counselor, writer, and teacher, this gifted communicator also conducts seminars around the country. His whole life is centered around speaking in one form or another. Who would've ever guessed that, growing up, this is the one thing he desperately wanted to avoid.

It seems Larry had a problem with stuttering when he was young. After a particularly humiliating experience in the ninth grade, he decided to shun all public speaking in the future. A short time later, however, he was pressured to pray in front of the congregation in his church. Listen to his memorable story.

> Filled less with worship than with nervousness,
> I found my theology becoming confused to the point
> of heresy. I remember thanking the Father for hanging on the cross and praising Christ for triumphantly
> bringing the Spirit from the grave. Stuttering throughout, I finally thought of the word *Amen* (perhaps the
> first evidence of the Spirit's leading), said it, and sat

down. I recall staring at the floor, too embarrassed to look around, and solemnly vowing *never again* to pray or speak aloud in front of a group. . . .

When the service was over, I darted toward the door, not wishing to encounter an elder who might feel obliged to correct my twisted theology. But I was not quick enough. An older Christian man named Jim Dunbar intercepted me, put his arm on my shoulder, and cleared his throat to speak.

I remember thinking to myself, "Here it comes. Oh well, just endure it and then get to the car." I then listened to this godly gentleman speak words that I can repeat verbatim today, more than twenty years later.

"Larry," he said, "there's one thing I want you to know. Whatever you do for the Lord, I'm behind you one thousand percent." Then he walked away.

Even as I write these words, my eyes fill with tears. I have yet to tell that story to an audience without at least mildly choking. Those words were life words. They had power. They reached deep into my being.[3]

God bless that man whose encouragement continues to directly benefit thousands through Larry Crabb's ministry today. Isn't that amazing? And yet, I bet if we were each to think back, we, too, could probably recall someone special who impacted our lives by their encouragement.

Who would that be for you? How have their words affected the course of your life?

_____

_____

_____

_____

We all hunger for "life words," as Larry put it. Most of us have tasted them before, but how much are we feeding others with them?

3. Crabb and Allender, *Encouragement: The Key to Caring*, pp. 24–25.

In the last week, whom have you made a conscious effort to encourage through a letter, a phone call, or a personal visit? Kind words cost us so little, yet why are we so miserly about giving them away?

Today, right now, spend some time in prayer asking God to sensitize you to those close to you who might need encouragement. As you pray, jot down whatever names come to mind and the kind of encouragement you sense they need.

_____

_____

_____

_____

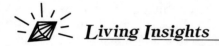 *Living Insights* _____ STUDY TWO

As you studied the lesson, did you sense the Holy Spirit's conviction in any particular one of the four good uses of the tongue? If so, write which use it was in the space provided.

_____

In what way were you convicted? Did you feel you should do more of something? Less? Was your thinking impacted in a way that made things more clear to you than ever before? Were you reminded of something you said recently that violated one of these principles? What?

This Living Insight isn't about doing what we want you to do, it's about listening and following the Holy Spirit's lead in what He wants you to do. If that's not clear yet, spend some time prayerfully rereading the passages where you felt His conviction. Ask Him to prompt within you the insight you need to understand His conviction and what to do about it. We'll leave you some space to record your thoughts.

_____

_____

_____

_____

Chapter 6

THE POISON
IN YOUR MOUTH
Selected Proverbs

But no one can tame the tongue; it is a restless evil
and full of deadly poison. (James 3:8)

In his exposition of this verse, Guy King put the tongue's poison
under the microscope of his focused study and made these important observations.

> The deadly drug does not need to be taken in large
> doses—a drop or two will suffice; and the tongue
> does not need to distil long speeches, it has but to
> drop a word, and the mischief is set afoot. Thus has a
> peace been ruined, thus has a reputation been black-
> ened, thus has a friendship been embittered, thus has
> a mind been poisoned, thus has a life been blasted.[1]

So deadly can the tongue be that Jesus issued one of the sternest
warnings in all of the New Testament concerning its use:

> "And I say to you, that every careless word that men
> shall speak, they shall render account for it in the
> day of judgment." (Matt. 12:36)

Sobering, isn't it? To think of all the things we said just yesterday
that will be repeated before the judgment throne of God puts real
panic in many of our hearts! And well it should. We're far too loose
with our words. But what are some of those "careless words" that
will one day come back to haunt us? Let's return to Proverbs for an
uncomfortable look at the wrong ways we wag our tongues.

Wrong Uses of the Tongue

Spouting folly, to use Solomon's term (see Prov. 15:2), can take
several unsavory forms.

---

1. Guy H. King, *A Belief That Behaves: An Expositional Study of the Epistle of James* (London,
England: Marshall, Morgan and Scott, 1941), p. 63.

Deceitful Flattery

> A lying tongue hates those it crushes,
> And a flattering mouth works ruin. (26:28)

Two different ways to define flattery are (1) insincere compliments given to gain favor or (2) excessive, undue praise. Either way, Solomon warns us not to use it or be used by it.

> He who hates disguises it with his lips,
> But he lays up deceit in his heart.
> When he speaks graciously, do not believe him.
> (vv. 24–25a)

Our speech is to be marked by sincerity and truth, not hypocrisy and falsehood.

Slander, Talebearing, and Gossip

Another use of the tongue that concerned Solomon has to do with the malicious circulation of false or exaggerated reports about another person.

> He who spreads slander is a fool. . . .
> He who goes about as a talebearer reveals secrets,
> But he who is trustworthy conceals a matter.
> (10:18b; 11:13)

Even revealing the truth at times can be nothing more than a sneaky way to slander someone else. Private conversations aired publicly can cause irreparable damage. Not everything we hear should be shared. One who "repeats a matter," Solomon warns, "separates intimate friends" (17:9b).

But aren't there times when information ought to be given that may not seem kind? Yes. For example, Jesus' heated rebuke of the Pharisees recorded in Matthew 23. Seven times He denounced the hypocrisy of their puffed-up piety. It was a direct reproof done with the right motive—to correct wrong—not a case of vicious slander meant simply to hurt someone.

The topic of talebearing often raises another, more difficult, question: *Aren't there times when confidential information ought to be shared?* Again, the answer is yes. Not that it happens very often, mind you. But there are times when it becomes legally or morally necessary to break a trust. Say a friend admits that he's involved in an adulterous relationship; what do you do? According to Matthew 18:15–17, he should first be confronted privately. If that fails, then he's to be confronted by two or three witnesses. If that also fails, the whole church is to be told and disciplinary action taken (see also 1 Tim. 5:19–20).

Other examples of when a trust should be broken involve child abuse or times when someone's life is in danger. Clearly, in these types of cases, confidentiality must be broken in order to protect the innocent. Even so, only those who absolutely need to know should be told.

More often than not, the difficulty we face is not with breaking confidentiality but with keeping it. So how can we restrain our lips? By forcing ourselves to answer these four exacting questions before we unleash our tongues.

- Is it true? If you can't check the source, then don't share it.

- Is it confidential? If so, then keep it under lock and key.

- Is it kind? Will it build up another? If not, don't say it.

- Is it necessary? Does this other person need to know this? If it won't make any difference, it's usually best left unsaid.

Arguments, Strife, and Angry Words

Has someone ever verbally given you a black eye? Was it a sarcastic sucker punch that got you? I thought so. We've all received some cheap shots like that. Solomon took his share of hits from hot-tempered jabberers, and he had this to say about them:

> A fool's lips bring strife,
> And his mouth calls for blows.
> A fool's mouth is his ruin,
> And his lips are the snare of his soul.
> (Prov. 18:6–7)

Listen to the Living Bible's perception of this same person.

> A fool gets into constant fights. His mouth is his undoing! His words endanger him.

A little later in 29:22, Solomon again describes a brawler.

> An angry man stirs up strife,
> And a hot-tempered man abounds in transgression.
> (29:22)

What do you do when you're thrown in the ring with such a

person at work or in church or out in the community? The worst thing you can do is clench your tongue and start swinging. For a more practical way to protect yourself, read 17:14.

> The beginning of strife is like letting out water,
> So abandon the quarrel before it breaks out.

It takes two to fight. So, the moment you sense that's where a conversation is headed, walk away—don't get into the ring. Refuse to mix it up by trading verbal punches.

Another way to fend off fights is found in 22:24–25.

> Do not associate with a man given to anger;
> Or go with a hot-tempered man,
> Lest you learn his ways,
> And find a snare for yourself.

When you meet someone who blasts out anger in a stream of molten words—keep going! Don't pursue a relationship with this kind of person. Especially if you're single and this individual wants to go out with you. Can you imagine anything more foolish or painful than marrying an angry person who constantly abuses you with his or her two-fisted words?

Boasting and Foolish Talking

The fool feels compelled to comment on everything. Her words flow in an incessant cascade of bubbling babble that signifies nothing. He always jockeys for the coveted position of having the last word—and the first—and most everything in between.

But not the wise. You won't hear her filling the air with empty prattle. He has mastered the crucial skill found in 17:27–28.

> He who restrains his words has knowledge,
> And he who has a cool spirit is a man of understanding.
> Even a fool, when he keeps silent, is considered wise;
> When he closes his lips, he is counted prudent.

Solomon depicts the folly of those who don't restrain their words in several different ways. For example, foolish jesting:

> He who mocks the poor reproaches his Maker;
> He who rejoices at calamity will not go unpunished.
> (17:5)

These days, many of the best-known comedians, male and female, constantly tell sick jokes about the misfortunes of others. They love to make us howl about adultery, poverty, murder, and perversion. And the truly sick part is, we're laughing.

A second trait of the fool is impulsiveness.

> He who gives an answer before he hears,
> It is folly and shame to him. (18:13)

Have you ever done this before? Somebody starts to make a point, and before he or she can finish, you jump in with both feet and start kicking and screaming to defend yourself. But when you finally quit fighting and listen to the rest of the story, you realize all you've done is stick both feet in your mouth? Embarrassing, wasn't it?

A third way we talk too much is with our boasting.

> Like clouds and wind without rain
> Is a man who boasts of his gifts falsely. (25:14)

The simplest way to avoid this mistake is to refrain from boasting altogether. Follow, instead, Solomon's advice:

> Let another praise you, and not your own mouth;
> A stranger, and not your own lips. (27:2)

Profanity and Vulgarity

Today, the airwaves are polluted with profanity. Television flaunts sexual immorality and innuendo. Hollywood continues to assault us with its nefarious penchant for pornography. Everywhere around us we see and hear this kind of crude folly. But this isn't simply the world's problem. Many Christians seem to have trouble breaking profane habits from their past. Far too many of us curse and laugh at lewd jokes, making our witness perhaps the biggest joke of all.

Perversion in the tongue, Solomon says, "crushes the spirit" (15:4). Maybe you grew up with a parent who cursed. Or perhaps you're working for someone now whose every other word is a mindless, obscene oath. It wears you down, doesn't it? You just get sick of hearing the filth that stains your memory, leaving you feeling unclean.

Unfortunately, the "kind of man whose teeth are like swords, And his jaw teeth like knives" (30:14a) is common in politics, sports, the military, among blue collar workers, business professionals, the entertainment industry, church softball leagues, and just about anywhere else you could name.

To the wise person, cursing is neither attractive nor fitting. It is juvenile and ugly; a pitifully base way to express ourselves. We have a choice, remember. "Death and life are in the power of the tongue" (18:21). Which are you wielding?

Lies and Exaggerations

The last wrong use of the tongue is found in Proverbs 6:16–19.

> There are six things which the Lord hates,
> Yes, seven which are an abomination to Him:
> Haughty eyes, a lying tongue,
> And hands that shed innocent blood,
> A heart that devises wicked plans,
> Feet that run rapidly to evil,
> A false witness who utters lies,
> And one who spreads strife among brothers.

Notice that out of the seven abominations the Lord hates, the tongue is mentioned three times. And twice specifically for lying! That *really* bothers our holy Father. So why doesn't it bother us as well? Why are we so lax about telling the truth, the whole truth, and nothing but the truth? Why is it that today a Christian's word is viewed with laughable contempt in many circles? It's because we've forgotten what it means to be holy, and we've adopted the relative values of the world we live in. So we lie, we fail to keep our word, we exaggerate, we try to cover up. But as Solomon warns us, and as experience has all too painfully proven,

> A false witness will not go unpunished,
> And he who tells lies will not escape. (19:5)

What could be more damning to our witness as bearers of the truth than our own lies? Speak the truth, practice it, handle it accurately. Remember that your word is a reflection not only of your character, but also of God's.

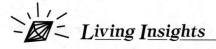 ***Living Insights*** STUDY ONE

Flattery—Slander—Strife—Boasting—Profanity—Lies
This is one sinister line-up of lawless words! Take a good look at each one. Do you recognize any of these rogues in yourself? See if you can identify the one verbal offender people are most likely

to hear from your lips.

In a way, you've just signed a confession. Now, the Law requires that you should be read your rights and booked. "You have the right to remain silent. Anything you say can and will be used against you." But this isn't a bust, so you needn't start worrying about bail. Besides, someone has already paid the "Wrongful Use" fine for your tongue long ago, so you're free to go.

That someone, of course, is Jesus (2 Cor. 5:21). Take a moment to thank Him, and then let's consider some specific steps to keep you out of trouble with this particular use of the tongue.

◆

Remember the four questions we recommended to interrogate your thoughts before they're released?

1. Is it true?
2. Is it confidential?
3. Is it kind?
4. Is it necessary?

I want you to think of the person or place that habitually tempts you to use your tongue in the way you confessed earlier. Got it? Now what's the first thing you can do to break this cycle so that you're not a repeat offender? No, it doesn't have anything to do with the questions—not yet. Think back to what Solomon said in Proverbs 22:24–25. Then read 1 Corinthians 15:33.

Now apply what you've just read to your situation. Do you need to stop associating with someone who's a bad influence? Is there a particular place you should avoid? That's the first step to consider.

But let's say you can't avoid a particular person or place. Maybe it's someone you work beside or carpool with or live next to. Now what? Now the questions. Now you've got to consciously, carefully begin to control the flow of your words by testing them first to see whether they are true, confidential, kind, or necessary.

Are you willing to put forth that effort? I think you'll be amazed at how much these questions can help and how quickly. Set aside a few minutes to take this matter before the Lord. Ask Him for a sensitivity to know when to apply those criteria and how. Then, in the space provided, keep track over the next few days of the different

ways this helps your tongue talk the straight and narrow.

_____

_____

_____

_____

_____

_____

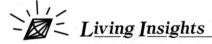 *Living Insights* STUDY TWO

My friend Rob Moore probably doesn't even remember the conversation. I'll never forget it.

It was years ago, before either one of us was married. We were rooming together, and I stopped him one day to talk about something I'd heard about someone else.

"Did you hear about . . . ?" I shared the news with my best "concerned Christian" face, but the truth is, I wasn't all that genuinely concerned. I was simply enjoying the smug satisfaction that comes from revealing all the illicit tidbits about someone else's mistakes. Right down to the last detail.

Rob listened patiently and then asked one question. *"How do you know that's true?"* The words left me speechless. Why? Because I suddenly realized that I didn't know if the story was true. I had no idea. Yet I had just related it to him as if it were.

About the only thing that was true in that embarrassing moment was my own hypocrisy. I hadn't been the least bit concerned with the accuracy of the story or, really, the person it was about. Gossip—guilty. Slander—guilty. Exaggeration—guilty.

Thanks, Rob Moore. I haven't forgotten the lesson you taught me. It has kept me from falling into the trap of gossiping about others countless times.

It could do the same for you if you'll ask yourself that same, unflinching question each time you're tempted to talk about someone else . . .

How do you know that's true?

Chapter 7

YOU AND YOUR JOB
(PART ONE)
Selected Proverbs

Do you do your best at work? Pursuing excellence is a rare commodity among many Americans today. Even rarer, it seems, and more disconcerting, is the number of Christians who actually do quality work. Our witness on the assembly line and in the office has become so disreputable that many personnel directors and presidents are now saying that they prefer *not* to hire Christians.

How many of you have felt that same disgust and distrust? How many times has it been the "trust me I'm a Christian," not the non-Christian, who has gone back on his or her word to you in business? Or defaulted on a debt? Or lied about the work that was done? Too many times, I suspect. And, undoubtedly, some of the individuals who ripped you off still proudly serve as deacons and elders in their churches.

This outrageous slandering of the name of Christ must be stopped! Could you imagine Moses shortchanging the shearers so he could have a little extra spending money for his return trip to Egypt? And what about Paul? Tent making was his trade. Is it likely he billed his clients for hours he never worked and then went out to tell people "Jesus saves"? Jesus was a carpenter. Do you think He was lazy? "I'm going to quit when I'm thirty anyway, so why bother?" Did He cut corners on quality and pass it off as "just business"? Of course not. Our work, like everything else, is a reflection of who we are and of the truth we proclaim. "Whatever you do," Paul wrote,

> do your work heartily, as for the Lord rather than
> for men; knowing that from the Lord you will receive
> the reward of the inheritance. It is the Lord Christ
> whom you serve. (Col. 3:23–24)

What's happened to that kind of work ethic among Christians? Why have we forsaken God's high calling to work hard? Perhaps it's time we took a close look at ourselves as employees in the mirror of Proverbs. In this lesson and the next, let's inspect the work force Solomon portrays to see if the habits and attitudes he's describing are our own.

Employees Nobody Wants

The initial group we'll interview consists of three undesirables no one wants to hire. Unfortunately, our first candidate canceled at the last moment—said something rather strange about a lion lurking near his home. But let's have a look at his qualifications anyway.

The Sluggard

> I passed by the field of the sluggard,
> And by the vineyard of the man lacking sense;
> And behold, it was completely overgrown with
>   thistles,
> Its surface was covered with nettles,
> And its stone wall was broken down.
> When I saw, I reflected upon it;
> I looked, and received instruction.
> "A little sleep, a little slumber,
> A little folding of the hands to rest,"
> Then your poverty will come as a robber,
> And your want like an armed man.
> (Prov. 24:30–34)

Sluggards come in all shapes and sizes—and denominations. Despite whatever creed they may claim, laziness is the only real on-the-job doctrine they vigorously practice. Each day they repeat the complainer's liturgy, which goes something like this: "What time is it? It's not my job. What time is it? I don't get paid enough to do this. What time is it—is it five o'clock yet?"

Beyond being a whiner, the sluggard is characterized by six other telltale signs.

1. *He has trouble getting started.*

> How long will you lie down, O sluggard?
> When will you arise from your sleep? (6:9)

Notice the two questions: *how long* and *when*. Couch potatoes who live by the motto "Never do today what you can put off until tomorrow" hate such pesky questions. Sure, they can tell you when all their favorite game shows begin, but tell you when they're going to start working on that leaky faucet they promised to fix? "Soon, real soon. I just need a little more rest . . . ZZZZZZZZZzz" (v. 10).

2. *She is restless—filled with inner plans she never implements.*

> The soul of the sluggard craves and gets nothing,
> But the soul of the diligent is made fat. . . .
> The desire of the sluggard puts him to death,
> For his hands refuse to work. (13:4; 21:25)

No clearer example of this can be found than in the life of Samuel Taylor Coleridge.

> Never did so great a mind produce so little. He left Cambridge University to join the army; he left the army because, in spite of all his erudition, he could not rub down a horse; he returned to Oxford and left without a degree. He began a paper called *The Watchman* which lived for ten numbers and then died. It has been said of him: "He lost himself in visions of work to be done, that always remained to be done. Coleridge had every poetic gift but one— the gift of sustained and concentrated effort." In his head and in his mind he had all kinds of books, as he said, himself, "completed save for transcription." . . . But the books were never composed outside Coleridge's mind, because he would not face the discipline of sitting down to write them out.[1]

"For his hands refused to work"—a poignant epitaph for a disappointing life.

3. *He is costly to the business.*

> He also who is slack in his work
> Is brother to him who destroys. (18:9)

Sluggards don't actually go around destroying things—they're too lazy for something so physically strenuous. But they do know how to destroy office morale with deadly gossip and how to turn profit into loss through slow productivity.

4. *She is often very defensive.*

> The sluggard is wiser in his own eyes
> Than seven men who can give a discreet answer.
> (26:16)

---

1. William Barclay, *The Gospel of Matthew*, vol. 1, rev. ed., The Daily Study Bible Series (Philadelphia, Pa.: Westminster Press, 1975), p. 280.

You'll never see a sluggard so animated as when she attempts to defend herself when confronted. Suddenly she's a paragon of virtue and industry, always right, always ready with a reason for everything, and deeply offended that you would dare question her work habits. Shame on you!

5. *He is a quitter.*

> A slothful man does not roast his prey,
> But the precious possession of a man is diligence.
> (12:27)

For you nonhunter types, the truth behind this proverb may seem about as clear as a deer in a thicket. What Solomon means is that the sluggard is too lazy to cook the game he kills. He may like to fish, for example, but he hates cleaning the catch. He starts out in all his endeavors with lots of enthusiasm, but then he fizzles for a nap before the work is finished.

6. *She lives under self-delusional excuses.*

> The sluggard says, "There is a lion outside;
> I shall be slain in the streets!" (22:13)

This is not your ordinary "I can't come in today, I'm sick" kind of excuse. Oh no. That's too banal for the self-respecting sluggard. The ancient lion-in-the-street ploy is melodramatic excuse making raised to an art form. And that's just what it is for most sluggards, who have a way of channeling all their creative energies into making excuses instead of a living.

Ah, Mr. Sluggard, what a surprise. I see you braved the lion to make it here after all. We just finished examining your resume, and I'm afraid we don't have any openings right now (or ever) for someone with your particular qualifications. If I may, however, I'd like to offer you two words of advice that may help you in the future. The first is found in Proverbs 6:6–8.

> Go to the ant, O sluggard,
> Observe her ways and be wise,
> Which, having no chief,
> Officer or ruler,
> Prepares her food in the summer,
> And gathers her provision in the harvest.

Remember the object lesson of the ant. It needs no boss to check up on it. It works hard in spite of the difficulties. And it plans ahead for the hard times. A wonderful example for you to emulate.

My second counsel is a word of warning. Remember, if you continue to fold your hands for "a little sleep, a little slumber," Solomon has said that "your poverty will come in like a vagabond, And your need like an armed man" (vv. 10–11).

The Deceiver

Solomon gives us a glimpse of our next interviewee in 11:18, a smooth, sweet-talking type:

> The wicked earns deceptive wages,
> But he who sows righteousness gets a true reward.

This is the employee who typically whispers things like, "No one will ever know," "Don't worry about it, everybody does it," and, "This is smart business. Besides, they owe it to me after all the hard work I've put into this company."

Have you ever worked with a deceiver before? Or maybe been conned by one wearing an *ichthus*[2] symbol and a "trust me, Brother" smile? I thought so. Most of us have, so let's see what helpful insights Solomon can give us about this worker of deceit.

1. *He appears to have a life of ease, but it's really empty and without purpose.*

> Wealth obtained by fraud dwindles. (13:11a)

The meaning of the Hebrew term for *wealth* has to do with more than just money. It also refers to what's "necessary to make life 'easy.'"[3] So it's the deceiver's "ease of life" that dwindles as his fraudulent activity continues. This same truth is reaffirmed a little later in 15:27a: "He who profits illicitly troubles his own house."

2. *The deception may be exciting initially, but its end is bitter and hard to bear.*

> Bread obtained by falsehood is sweet to a man,
> But afterward his mouth will be filled with gravel.
> (20:17)

2. An *ichthus* is "a representation of a fish used in ancient times . . . as a Christian symbol for the Greek word *ichthys* interpreted as an acrostic in which the Greek letters are the initials of the words Iesous Christos theou hyios sōtēr meaning Jesus Christ Son of God Savior." See *Webster's Third New International Dictionary of the English Language Unabridged* (Springfield, Mass.: Merriam-Webster, Inc.), 1981, p. 1121.

3. R. Laird Harris, Gleason L. Archer, Jr., and Bruce K. Waltke, eds., *Theological Wordbook of the Old Testament* (Chicago, Ill.: Moody Press, 1980), vol. 1, p. 213.

Don't let anyone tell you that sin doesn't exhilarate. It does. Successfully stealing something produces a twisted kind of "high." You feel cocky and lucky and excited all at the same time. And it's not only the professional thief who experiences such feelings; it's everyone who steals, from the office worker who pilfers pens and paper clips to the president who siphons off thousands every year. Like all emotions, however, that fugitive feeling soon steals away, leaving in its place the gritty taste of reality—guilt, shame, and a deadness of spirit.

Do you pay for everything you take home from your job?

3. *He lacks a sense of loyalty.*

> Like a bad tooth and an unsteady foot
> Is confidence in a faithless man in time of
>   trouble. (25:19)

The deceiver is also disloyal. You can't count on him. He'll be one of the first to abandon ship and leave you stranded when hard times hit.

You can come in now, Mr. Deceiver. I've examined your resume and—pardon me? Oh, thank you. I've always liked this tie too. As I was saying—excuse me? Yes, I noticed the *ichthus* on your lapel. If I could just—you mentored Francis Schaeffer? Amazing. Even so, "Brother," I'm afraid your talents just don't fit the needs of this company. Perhaps if you were to follow Paul's advice in Ephesians 4:28, you'd keep your next job and never have to apply for another.

> Let him who steals steal no longer; but rather let
> him labor, performing with his own hands what is
> good, in order that he may have something to share
> with him who has need.

The Greedy

Our last applicant to review is presented to us in Proverbs 28:22.

> A man with an evil eye hastens after wealth,
> And does not know that want will come upon
>   him.

People who chase after riches say things like, "When I make my first million . . . " and, "All I need is just a little bit more, and then I'll quit, I promise." Of course, they never do. Work is number one for these people. Marriage, family, serving others—none of these matter as much as making a buck. But that's not all. Let's dig a little deeper into this person's background by reading still more from Solomon's personnel files in Proverbs.

1. *He attempts to find security in money.*

> He who trusts in his riches will fall,
> But the righteous will flourish like the green leaf.
> (11:28)

Money satisfies. It holds the key to real happiness. Or so the greedy believe with religious fervor. But they worship a paper god that can never give what the priests of marketing promise (see Eccles. 5:10).

2. *She never slows her fanatical pursuit of riches.*

> Do not weary yourself to gain wealth,
> Cease from your consideration of it.
> When you set your eyes on it, it is gone.
> For wealth certainly makes itself wings,
> Like an eagle that flies toward the heavens.
> (Prov. 23:4–5)

Despite all promises and warnings, the greedy often refuse to abandon their quest for the pot of gold at the end of the rainbow. Even those who obtain the riches they set out to find soon discover that, instead of lasting satisfaction and joy, they now feel a new discontent that drives them to work even harder and make even more.

3. *He is extremely selfish.* Jesus pictured this aspect of the greedy person in a parable.

> "The land of a certain rich man was very productive. And he began reasoning to himself, saying, 'What shall I do, since I have no place to store my crops?' And he said, 'This is what I will do: I will tear down my barns, and build larger ones, and there I will store all my grain and my goods. And I will say to my soul, "Soul, you have many goods laid up for many years to come; take your ease, eat, drink and be merry."' But God said to him, 'You fool! This very night your soul is required of you; and now who will own what you have prepared?'" . . . And [Jesus] said to them, "Beware, and be on your guard against every form of greed; for not even when one

has an abundance does his life consist of his possessions." (Luke 12:16–20, 15)

Like the rich man, all greedy individuals measure their lives by the treasures they hoard. Selfishness consumes their every motive, act, and relationship.

4. *She will get burned because of her greed.*

> A faithful man will abound with blessings,
> But he who makes haste to be rich will not go
> unpunished. (Prov. 28:20)

Greed rewards its followers with loneliness, broken marriages, alienated children, lots of enemies, drug abuse, emptiness, prison, and, at times, even suicide.

Well, I think that tells us all we need to know about this kind of employee. I'm sorry, Mr. Greedy, but I'm afraid we won't be able to hire you, either. Let me encourage you to read the *entire* book of Ecclesiastes. It was written by a wealthy individual I'm sure you'll admire, whose advice may help you rethink some of your financial goals. Perhaps then you could come back and we'll reconsider your application. Oh, I see . . . you think God can best use a humble servant like yourself ministering to the rich.

Uh-oh!

Living Insights

As you looked in Solomon's mirror at the sluggard, the deceiver, and the greedy, did any of what you saw reflect the way you behave as an employee? For far too many Christians, the likeness is uncomfortably accurate. Why? What makes our witness at work resemble one of those three characters instead of Christ?

In their excellent book *Your Work Matters to God*, authors Doug Sherman and William Hendricks answer that question with this important insight.

> At the beginning of creation, work may have started out in a garden. But in our generation it has ended up in a jungle. . . .
> . . . Work has become warlike, as workers seek competitive advantage over others. To survive and prevail requires "intimidating friends and seducing

people." Consequently, distractions such as moral scruples must be left behind when one enters the jungle. A sort of moral Darwinism rules there: Survival depends on doing not what is right, but what works.

. . . In such a jungle, it seems predictable that [the worker] will do *whatever* it takes to achieve his goals:

> What is good is what one finds rewarding. If one's preferences change, so does the nature of the good. Even the deepest ethical virtues are justified as matters of personal preference. Indeed, the ultimate ethical rule is simply that individuals should be able to pursue whatever they find rewarding, constrained only by the requirement that they not interfere with the "value systems" of others. [Bellah, et al., *Habits of the Heart*, p. 6]

This nullifies lasting commitment to anyone or anything outside of oneself. If a relationship (spouse, child, friend, subordinate) stands in the way, one sacrifices it. If a boss or board obstructs one's progress, one goes to work undercover. If legal or moral issues prove bothersome, one compromises them. All on the basis of expediency.

Such a principle is purely secular in that the individual himself not only sets his goals, but sets his rules as well. He sees no authority or value system higher than himself to which he will ultimately submit.[4]

Even Christians? Yes, even Christians. We have forgotten Paul's admonition that it is the Lord Christ whom we serve, not expediency. Somehow we have separated our work from the reach of God's rules, and we play by the laws of the jungle instead. That's why the world often can't discern any difference between the Christian and the non-Christian in the workplace.

Is your behavior on the job governed by what works instead of by what's right? Do you do whatever it takes to get results, even if that means bending the truth or breaking a few rules?

---

4. Doug Sherman and William Hendricks, *Your Work Matters to God* (Colorado Springs, Colo.: NavPress, 1987), pp. 31–32.

"But that's just business. Everybody does it." Hmmm. Now where have we heard that before?

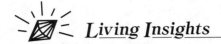 ## *Living Insights*

This may hurt a little.

Now I realize none of us likes having to admit to weaknesses or mistakes. And I also know that it would be a lot more fun to just sit back and criticize those three workers from the lesson. But that's not the shot in the arm we need to correct some of our own mistakes. To do that we've got to painstakingly examine ourselves in the light of the characteristics we noted about the sluggard, the deceiver, and the greedy.

If it will make you feel any better, I'll go first.

Do I have trouble getting started?

Sometimes I do have trouble getting started. It seems to happen most when several big things stack up on me all at the same time. I start feeling overwhelmed, and then do you know what I do? "A little sleep, a little slumber, a little folding of the hands." That's right, I rack out. I just shut the world out and hibernate.

There now, that wasn't so bad. Now it's your turn. Look through each of the characteristics and jot down any of your own weaknesses.

Am I restless—filled with inner plans I never implement?

Am I costly to my business?

58

Am I often defensive?

_____

_____

_____

Am I a quitter?

_____

_____

_____

Do I constantly make excuses for my sloppy work?

_____

_____

_____

Do I lack a sense of loyalty?

_____

_____

_____

Am I attempting to find security in money?

_____

_____

_____

*Am I extremely self-centered about the way
I spend and seek to earn more money?*

_____

_____

_____

Finally, what counsel have you gleaned from Proverbs or elsewhere that can help you improve?

For me, I'm learning how to break down big problems into bite-sized chunks. That way I get started quicker without experiencing sleepiness brought on by acute panic!

Chapter 8

YOU AND YOUR JOB
(PART TWO)
Selected Proverbs

Next!

We're ready to begin our second round of interviews, drawing once again from the pool of applicants in Proverbs. This time, however, our focus will be on the *right* kind of worker.

Employees Everybody Wants

Fortunately, not all Christians are sluggards, deceivers, or greed-mongers. Many do their work heartily as unto the Lord, leaving behind on every job an unmistakable calling card about their character and their God. We're about to meet three such respected workers. Ah, here comes the first one . . . right on time as usual.

The Diligent

Please, come in and have a seat. Let's look at the qualifications Solomon lists about you.

> Poor is he who works with a negligent hand,
> But the hand of the diligent makes rich. (Prov. 10:4)

The Hebrew term for *diligent* can mean "to cut or sharpen." It's used here to connote the kind of worker who is sharp, decisive, keen—three impressive traits that would grab any employer's attention. Adding to these, Solomon gives four other outstanding recommendations.

1. *He shows discipline and determination.* Both of these qualities are readily visible in the diligent. He is steady, earnest, and enthusiastic. He knows how to avoid distractions and make good use of his time. You can depend on him to handle situations with efficiency. He accomplishes his goals.

2. *She demonstrates an alert awareness.* This, too, is implied by the Hebrew term for *diligent* in verse 4. She is perceptive, on top of things, able to anticipate what to do without having to be told every step of the way.

3. *He is a rare and valuable find.*

> A slothful man does not roast his prey,
> But the precious possession of a man is diligence.
> (12:27)

The term for *precious* suggests rarity. Diligent workers are as rare a find in the workplace as precious gems are in nature. Employers must usually dig at considerable cost to uncover an individual whose performance shines with this prized quality.

4. *She is a reservoir of plans and ideas.*

> The plans of the diligent lead surely to
>   advantage,
> But everyone who is hasty comes surely to
>   poverty. (21:5)

According to the *Theological Wordbook of the Old Testament*, the basic idea of the word *plans* is "the employment of the mind in thinking activity. Reference is not so much to 'understanding' . . . , but to the creating of new ideas."[1] Diligent individuals are oftentimes innovative thinkers, constantly creating and shaping new ideas.

As valuable as these traits may be to an employer, it is also important to realize their worth to employees. They, too, are recompensed, as Solomon notes in 12:11:

> He who tills his land will have plenty of bread,
> But he who pursues vain things lacks sense.

Though this is not a blanket, absolute promise, the principle Solomon gives here does generally hold true. Those who work diligently in whatever "field" they find themselves will typically reap an adequate harvest to provide for their needs.

A few thoughts later, in verse 24, Solomon implies that the diligent will also be promoted above those who are like the sluggard.

> The hand of the diligent will rule,
> But the slack hand will be put to forced labor.

And, finally, we're told that diligence brings with it a feast of inner satisfaction.

---

1. R. Laird Harris, Gleason L. Archer, Jr., and Bruce K. Waltke, eds., *Theological Wordbook of the Old Testament* (Chicago, Ill.: Moody Press, 1980), vol. 1, p. 330.

The soul of the sluggard craves and gets nothing,
But the soul of the diligent is made fat. . . .
Desire realized is sweet to the soul. (13:4, 19a)

Every disciplined and determined worker relishes the satisfying taste of accomplishment. The natural high that comes from meeting a deadline and finishing a project motivates and lightens our hearts, rather than weighing us down with guilt and regret.

Well, Ms. Diligent, I think we've seen enough to know that you're just the person we've been looking for to oversee some of our operations. When can you start?

The Thoughtful

Actually, we have two kinds of thoughtful workers to consider from Proverbs. Let's start with what makes a *thoughtful boss*.

1. *She is genuinely concerned about the lives of her employees.*

A righteous man has regard for the life of his
      beast,
But the compassion of the wicked is cruel. (12:10)

At first glance, this proverb may seem to have little to do with an employer, but think about it. How many bosses have you known who treated their employees as if they were lowly beasts of burden whose only worth was measured by the load they could carry? More than a few, I suspect. A righteous person, a thoughtful employer, however, shows a genuine concern and compassion for the employee. This same principle is reaffirmed a little later in 27:23.

Know well the condition of your flocks,
And pay attention to your herds.

Isn't it interesting that after years of distancing themselves from their employees, management in corporate America has finally recognized the value of this "thoughtful employer" principle? Companies have been revolutionized by it. Business experts have written books and given seminars to teach this newfound secret of effective management. Only it's not new—this same principle has been patiently waiting to be rediscovered for nearly three thousand years!

2. *He has understanding and insight.*

Like a roaring lion and a rushing bear
Is a wicked ruler over a poor people.

> A leader who is a great oppressor lacks
> understanding. (28:15–16a)

This word picture reproachfully compares the cruel, belligerent tyrant to the most dangerous animals known. Turn it around, though, and we'll find that its opposite is also true: A good leader who resists trampling others with his power has understanding. People don't fear such a boss. They don't run and hide every time he passes, dreading a malicious attack. Instead, they enjoy his presence and instinctively follow his lead.

In the hands of a thoughtful employer, work becomes a place of ministry, an opportunity to build into the lives of others. And the benefit? Those who work *for* you will begin to work *with* you.

The second worker to consider in this category is the *thoughtful employee.*

> He who tends the fig tree will eat its fruit;
> And he who cares for his master will be honored.
> (27:18)

Every thoughtful employee possesses at least two essential traits. (1) He is committed to his job—"tends the fig tree"; and (2) she is loyal to her employer—"cares for his master." Practice these qualities, Solomon says, and the job will yield enjoyable fruit and honor will come your way.

Mr. Thoughtful Employer and Mrs. Thoughtful Employee, your records are impeccable, and it would be a tremendous asset to hire you both. When can you start?

The Skillful

> Do you see a man skilled in his work?
> He will stand before kings;
> He will not stand before obscure men. (22:29)

Think about your own job for a moment. If someone had looked over your shoulder last week, would that individual have witnessed someone who is skilled in his or her work? Are you efficient? Do you possess the technical expertise to carry out your job with competence? Perhaps you need to brush up on new technology, take a refresher course, read a book, or maybe just put more effort into what you do, whether it's being a homemaker, draftsman, plumber, printer, secretary, mechanic, or waitress.

The world desperately needs to see Christians who are skilled in their vocations. That one quality alone will open doors for us to receive respect and a good reputation among non-Christians— doors that might never be opened as wide in any other way. What an impact that would have on the world! It gives a broader meaning to Jesus' words: "Let your light shine before men in such a way that they may see your good [skilled] works, and glorify your Father who is in heaven" (Matt. 5:16).

When can you start?

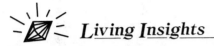 **Living Insights**

Many of us have felt like George Bailey, the main character in the film classic *It's a Wonderful Life*.[2] George has grand visions for his life that always somehow get thwarted, leaving him feeling chained to a very ordinary existence in his little hometown of Bedford Falls.

Finally, in exasperation over a calamity that threatens to close his business and ruin his reputation, George wishes he'd never been born. His wish is granted, and through a frightening barrage of discoveries, he sees how significant his "ordinary" life has actually been. George's diligent, thoughtful, and skillful work at his humble savings and loan impacted many lives and changed the course of the entire town for good.

Like George, many Christians tend to label their lives and activities as important or ordinary, spiritual or secular. Pastoring a church, for example, is important work. Being an electrician isn't. Mission work is spiritual. Stocking food in a grocery store is secular.

But do the Scriptures really teach this kind of categorizing? In their outstanding book *Your Work Matters to God*, authors Doug Sherman and William Hendricks counter this false division.

> There is no distinction between the secular and the sacred. At any moment, no matter what we are doing, we are relating to God either properly or improperly. Thus we need to distinguish, not between secular and sacred, but between sin and righteousness.

2. This Living Insight has been adapted from the study guide *Questions Christians Ask*, coauthored by Lee Hough, from the Bible-teaching ministry of Charles R. Swindoll (Fullerton, Calif.: Insight for Living, 1989), pp. 57–58.

In other words, you can go to church and pray (a "sacred" category) and yet still be in sin. You may recite a creed or partake of the elements yet retain hateful thoughts toward someone who has wronged you. Or sit there and dream about your ambitions, and how fulfilling them will give you esteem, power, or money. . . .

On the other hand, you can go to work in an office where the atmosphere is very "secular"—the conversation is littered with profanity, the jokes are off-color, the work is often slipshod, the politics are wearisome. And yet, like Daniel or Joseph in the Old Testament, you can keep your own conversation pure and your behavior above reproach. You can do your work with integrity, even if others do not. You can honor and obey God in a very worldly environment.

In short, God's interest is not simply that we do holy activities but that we become holy people. Not pious. Not sanctimonious. Not other-worldly. But pure, healthy, Christlike.[3]

Does this biblical perspective challenge or affirm the way you view your work? In what ways?

_____

_____

_____

_____

_____

_____

_____

Like George Bailey, your life and your work make a difference . . . in ways you may never know.

3. Doug Sherman and William Hendricks, *Your Work Matters to God* (Colorado Springs, Colo.: NavPress, 1987), pp. 54–55.

Living Insights

I don't think I'll ever forget it. It was windy, bitter cold, and there I was digging in a ditch in downtown Dallas. People in immaculate three-piece power suits and designer dresses swirled past me like I was just a part of the shrubbery we were putting in. The only people who did seem to notice me were the con men and the derelicts. Everywhere I looked—the limousines, the towers of polished granite, the designer boutiques, the leather briefcases—everything flaunted success and purpose at a time when I felt utterly a failure, without any purpose.

It was a period of deep testing in my life. In an earlier time, in a more comfortable setting, I had vigorously defended the truth that we can glorify God with our work no matter how mundane or insignificant the world may deem it. But now my wife was pregnant, we were living out of a suitcase from one friend's house to the next, and I barely made enough pushing that dirt around to even buy groceries.

Suddenly all that talk about "whatever you do, do your work heartily as for the Lord" hung in the balance. Mere words or solid truth to sustain me in my worst nightmare? Now was my chance to find out. Dig holes with diligence? Be thoughtful knee-deep in dirt on a crowded sidewalk? Weld with skill an iron grating beneath the ground that no one would ever see?

Maybe you're struggling as I was in your job right now. Perhaps it's not glamorous. It may even be monotonous or seemingly insignificant in comparison to what you see others doing around you. Will you still do your work heartily as for the Lord?

Brainstorm some practical ways you can exhibit each of the three qualities studied in the lesson.

Diligence

_____

_____

_____

_____

_____

_____

Thoughtfulness

_____

_____

_____

_____

_____

_____

Skillfulness

_____

_____

_____

_____

_____

_____

Chapter 9

YOU AND YOUR COUNSELING

(PART ONE)

Selected Proverbs

Would you call yourself a counselor? Most of us wouldn't; not unless we have earned an advanced degree in psychology and are licensed to practice. Nowadays even many pastors defer counseling to those considered to be "trained professionals."

Granted, in certain cases it is best to rely on professionals skilled at untying particular mental or emotional knots. But is it necessary all the time? Are we being too quick to disqualify ourselves as capable counselors for many of life's everyday tangles?

The apostle Paul thought so. Listen to his words from Romans 15.

> As far as I am concerned about you, my brothers,
> I am convinced that you especially are abounding
> in the highest goodness, richly supplied with perfect
> knowledge and competent to counsel one another.
> (Rom. 15:14 WILLIAMS)

The Apostle wasn't addressing a convention of psychotherapists here; he was speaking to all the Christians in Rome, many of whom were slaves. So what did he mean by *counsel?* Let's turn to the Old Testament to find out.

What Is Meant by "Counseling" in the Old Testament?

Throughout the Law and the Prophets, the writers used basically four Hebrew words to signify *counsel, counseling,* and *counselor.*

1. *Dabar* (pronounced "dah-baar"). This word is occasionally translated *counsel* (see Num. 31:16). Most often, however, it indicates ordinary, everyday talking, as in Deuteronomy 11:18–19.

> "You shall therefore impress these words of mine
> on your heart and on your soul; and you shall bind
> them as a sign on your hand, and they shall be as
> frontals on your forehead. And you shall teach them
> to your sons, *talking* of them when you sit in your

house and when you walk along the road and when you lie down and when you rise up." (emphasis added)

Parents needn't wait for trained professionals in the church to expose their children to biblical truth. They are to *dabar* their children in the normal over-the-dinner-table, around-the-home, and out-in-the-neighborhood conversations. Much of what passes for normal exchanges among family members and friends is actually a low-key form of counseling.

2. *Sod* ("sahd"). A second term with a slightly different shade of meaning is found in the first half of Proverbs 15:22.

> Without *consultation*, plans are frustrated,
> But with many counselors they succeed.
> (emphasis added)

"Consultation," translated *sod*, means "being brought close together for the purpose of secret communication and counsel."[1] It differs from *dabar* in that an ingredient of confidentiality has been added. When someone asks to speak to you privately about a matter, that's *sod*.

3. *Chabal* ("cha-bahl"). Another term for *counsel* is used in 1:5:

> A wise man will hear and increase in learning,
> And a man of understanding will acquire wise counsel.

The word Solomon uses for "counsel" comes from the root term *chabal*, meaning "to bind or to pledge." Originally, this word was used of "*rope*-pulling, i.e. *steering, directing* a ship."[2] It's the idea of giving specific direction to someone, pulling that person along with a binding agreement or project to correct his or her course.

4. *Yaats* ("yah-ahtz"). The next term, found in 12:20, is used more widely than any other.

> Deceit is in the heart of those who devise evil,
> But counselors of peace have joy.

1. C. F. Keil and F. Delitzsch, *Commentary on the Old Testament* (reprint; Grand Rapids, Mich.: William B. Eerdmans Publishing Co., 1978), vol. 6, p. 328.

2. William Gesenius, *A Hebrew and English Lexicon of the Old Testament*, trans. Edward Robinson, ed. Francis Brown, S. R. Driver, Charles A. Briggs (Oxford, England: Clarendon Press, n.d.), p. 287.

A popular counseling technique today defines the counselor's role as one of neutral observation, someone who simply listens and reflects what the other person is saying—without making any judgments or offering any advice. Certainly, counselors need to listen and gather information at the beginning. But then to sit there, knowing the help this other person needs but not telling him or her is completely foreign to the biblical view of counseling. To give wise *yaats* means sharing direct, objective information.

The New Testament equivalent is *noutheteō*, "admonish" (Rom. 15:14), which means "to put into the mind." That's what counseling involves—imparting truth to the minds of troubled and confused individuals.

Combining the meanings of all four words into one definition, we might say this:

> *Counseling involves communicating with someone for the purpose of clarifying, instructing, or changing areas of his or her life that need attention.*

Occasionally, this is done in a formal setting with a professional. More often, however, it occurs informally in the casual exchanges of everyday living: friends clarifying issues for friends; parents instructing children; one person impacting another by something he says or she does, sometimes without even knowing it.

Does Counseling Yield Specific Benefits?

For years, the Christian community has been leery of counseling. We have shunned this practice out of fear and ignorance. Solomon, however, understood its positive benefits and mentions at least four in Proverbs.

First, *to help heal and relieve anxiety.*

> There is one who speaks rashly like the thrusts of
> a sword,
> But the tongue of the wise brings healing. . . .
> Anxiety in the heart of a man weighs it down,
> But a good word makes it glad. (12:18, 25)

No one can escape the bumps and bruises that come from living in a fallen world. But the tongue of the wise can act like a balm, therapeutic and soothing. It strengthens our inner spirits to fight the infection of anxiety.

Second, *to help us find maximum fulfillment in life*.

> Where there is no guidance, the people fall,
> But in abundance of counselors there is victory.
> (11:14)

Everyone's perspective is limited. Wise counsel from a variety of viewpoints provides a fuller, more accurate picture of the options available in our lives. The wisdom and insight of good friends can blow away the fog of self-doubt, opening our eyes to possibilities God has in store for us (see Eph. 3:20). They can show us the way to make our hopes come true and our lives fulfilled.

> Hope deferred makes the heart sick,
> But desire fulfilled is a tree of life. (Prov. 13:12)

Third, *to help us plan correctly*.

> Without consultation, plans are frustrated,
> But with many counselors they succeed. . . .
> Prepare plans by consultation,
> And make war by wise guidance. (15:22; 20:18)

Are you seeking God's will about something important? A career move? A marriage choice? A business decision? Is there someone in your life who, for some unknown reason, has declared war on you? Someone you need to proceed with caution around? You aren't the first person to struggle through such issues, so be wise! Draw from the vast pool of counselors whose experience can guide you in what paths to take . . . and which to avoid.

Fourth, *to help us become wise, to see life through the lens of God's divine viewpoint*.

> Through presumption comes nothing but strife,
> But with those who receive counsel is wisdom. . . .
> Listen to counsel and accept discipline,
> That you may be wise the rest of your days.
> (13:10; 19:20)

How skewed our world's perspective is when it applauds as "confident" and "sure of themselves" those who presume to know what's best for them—apart from God's input. Their lives are scarred and circumvented by their own foolish thinking and choices; frustration and bitterness batter their spirits.

But when we are humble, open to the truth of our need and responsive toward change, then wisdom and its rewards define our days. Seeking and being receptive to counsel is the thing to commend—save ridicule for presumption.

Which Ingredients Make Some Counselors More Effective Than Others?

Let's benefit from more of Solomon's wisdom by examining eight traits of an effective counselor from the book of Proverbs. We'll cover the first five in the remainder of this chapter and the final three in the next.

Purity of Life

Young and old, Christians needing wisdom should seek out those who are skilled in godly living.

> But the path of the righteous is like the light of
>   dawn,
> That shines brighter and brighter until the full day.
> The way of the wicked is like darkness;
> They do not know over what they stumble.
> (4:18–19)

People respect a pure life because it gives off a light that attracts those who are lost and confused. Walk in the Spirit and you won't have to hang a shingle; the weary and heavy-laden will beat a path to your door.

Confidentiality

We touched on this same issue earlier, remember, in the chapter dealing with the wrong uses of the tongue.

> He who goes about as a talebearer reveals secrets,
> But he who is trustworthy conceals a matter. . . .
> Argue your case with your neighbor,
> And do not reveal the secret of another.
> (11:13; 25:9)

One of the most basic requirements of a good counselor is a closed mouth. Confidentiality breeds security and trust, essentials that foster freedom in communicating. If you're a name-dropper, if you can't bury forever information that is shocking or scandalous, then you're not qualified to have others share their personal short-comings and hurts with you. An effective counselor respects the power of information and wields it with extreme discretion.

Timing and Tact

A third quality of a good counselor is found in 15:23 and 28.

> A man has joy in an apt answer,
> And how delightful is a timely word! . . .
> The heart of the righteous ponders how to answer,
> But the mouth of the wicked pours out evil things.

The timing of a word is often as important as the words themselves. Competent counselors are patient, slow to speak, and quick to listen. They wait for the appropriate moment to give a precise word of counsel instead of insensitively dumping everything they know on someone the first moment there's a pause.

In addition to knowing when to speak, worthy counselors also ponder how to say things. They understand the power of words and carefully craft each question and response.

Keen Attention and Concentration

> He who gives an answer before he hears,
> It is folly and shame to him. (18:13)

When was the last time you were in a conversation with someone who kept interrupting you? You've met the kind. They can hardly wait—sometimes *don't* wait—for you to finish talking so they can begin pontificating. They're really not interested in your thoughts or feelings, only in espousing their own.

A quality counselor, however, is a good listener. He looks you in the eye, not over the shoulder or around the room. She concentrates, blocking out all other distractions so she can hear what's being said, as well as what's not being said. They probe, ask clarifying questions, seek to understand so they can offer true empathy and accurate advice.

Objectivity and Discernment

An effective counselor also avoids the trap of making snap judgments based on first impressions.

> The first to plead his case seems just,
> Until another comes and examines him. (v. 17)

Objectivity waits to hear both sides of the story. It allows discernment to search below the surface to find the root issues. "Pretty words may hide a wicked heart," Solomon wrote, "just as a pretty glaze covers a common clay pot" (26:23 LB). Perceptive counselors are not easily sidetracked. They know how to get past the glaze of our self-protection to touch the common clay of our painful needs or our sinful humanity.

As you can tell by now, it takes more than just technical skill to be an effective counselor. The qualities we've examined are ones we can all possess without having to attend graduate school. Before we consider the remaining traits in the next chapter, let's pause to reflect on the truths covered so far.

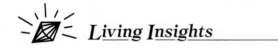 **_Living Insights_**

"Mr. Thompson, I believe I've finally pinpointed your problem. You're suffering from posttraumatic potty training. I can see now that you're the victim of terrible abuse. No wonder you can't control your anger. I think we can build a case here for temporary insanity and get the manslaughter charges dropped in exchange for six months therapy."

That's counseling. Or so some people think. We actually do see this kind of outrageous, psychobabble excuse-making happening all the time, but it has nothing to do with the biblical concept of counseling.

The real benefit of wise counseling is not to remove personal responsibility by blaming our past for our present behavior. Nor is it simply to make us happy—cheerful adulterers, contented frauds, or merry alcoholics. What do you think should be the overarching benefit or goal of Christian counseling? Of your counsel to others? In one or two words, sum up what you find in each of the following passages, then write down a composite definition from what you learned from them.

Romans 12:1–2 _____

Ephesians 4:20–24; 5:1–2 _____

Philippians 1:9–10 _____

Colossians 1:28 _____

Hebrews 6:1a _____

1 Peter 1:14–16 _____

Composite Definition

_____

_____

_____

_____

Living Insights

Take a moment to measure your own effectiveness as a counselor using the five traits from our study in Proverbs. On a scale from one to ten, one being the weakest, circle the number that best represents the strength or weakness of each trait in you.

Purity of Life

1   2   3   4   5   6   7   8   9   10

Confidentiality

1   2   3   4   5   6   7   8   9   10

Timing and Tact

1   2   3   4   5   6   7   8   9   10

Keen Attention and Concentration (A Good Listener)

1   2   3   4   5   6   7   8   9   10

Objectivity and Discernment

1   2   3   4   5   6   7   8   9   10

Using the same scale, what number would you choose to signify the overall effectiveness of your counseling?_____

Finally, beside each trait, write the name of the biblical character (a different one for each) who you feel best models that quality.

Chapter 10

YOU AND YOUR
COUNSELING
(PART TWO)

Selected Proverbs

Just as our physical bodies need water, so our invisible inner souls
need understanding. We thirst for it in our spirits. It is one of
our deepest longings, one that we constantly seek to quench. And
each time someone gives us a drink from its cup, our hearts are
refreshed.

Effective counselors are a well of understanding to those who
come to them. Let's explore this sixth quality and the remaining
two in our list of traits of an effective counselor. As with our
previous chapter, we'll rely on Solomon's help, as we once again
turn to his book of Proverbs.

More Qualities That Make Us Effective Counselors

Understanding

> As in water face reflects face,
> So the heart of man reflects man. (Prov. 27:19)

Commentators Keil and Delitzsch draw out the meaning of this
verse for us:

> The thought is beautiful: as in the water-mirror each
> one beholds his own face . . . , so out of the heart
> of another each sees his own heart, *i.e.* he finds in
> another the dispositions and feelings of his own
> heart . . . the face finds in water its reflection, and
> the heart of a man finds in man its echo; . . . it is
> a fortunate thing that their heart is capable of the
> same sympathetic feelings, so that one can pour into
> the heart of another that which fills and moves his
> own heart, and can there find . . . a re-echo.[1]

---

1. C. F. Keil and F. Delitzsch, *Commentary on the Old Testament* (reprint; Grand Rapids,
Mich.: William B. Eerdmans Publishing Co., 1978), vol. 6, pp. 214–15.

How exactly can we communicate this gift of understanding? The first of two significant attitudes that convey it is *acceptance*. Now, this doesn't necessarily mean approving of what someone has done or said or plans to do. It simply means loving the person; showing the same kind of unconditional love God pours out on us all, sinner and saint alike.

Unfortunately, many of us exude rejection more than acceptance. We constantly pass judgment on others with harsh words like, "You're just a troublemaker," or, "He got what he deserved," or, "She'll never learn. Helping her is just a waste of time." Rejection kills the spirit of the one giving it as well as the one receiving it. We should learn, instead, to accept, to affirm the God-given value instilled in every human being no matter who they are or what they've done.

A second way to communicate understanding is through a *willingness to get involved*. The uninvolved look around the room, say "hello" to passersby, or continue doing piddly work while you talk. But you can usually tell a person of understanding simply by reading his or her eyes, posture, and words. They invite you in, encourage you to unburden yourself, reaffirm that they care and want to help.

Honesty

The seventh crucial characteristic is found in 24:23–26.

> These also are sayings of the wise.
> To show partiality in judgment is not good.
> He who says to the wicked, "You are righteous,"
> Peoples will curse him, nations will abhor him;
> But to those who rebuke the wicked will be delight,
> And a good blessing will come upon them.
> He kisses the lips
> Who gives a right answer.

This particular passage reminded Chuck of a painfully heated counseling session he had once with a young couple. When it was over, the wife wiped the tears from her eyes and said, "Thank you for telling us the truth, for being honest. I hated you for it at the time . . . but I would have hated you more if you'd have fudged. We needed to hear the truth."

In the final analysis, people who really want help will appreciate your telling them the truth. Solomon affirmed this when he wrote,

He who rebukes a man will afterward find more favor
Than he who flatters with the tongue. (28:23)

Speak the truth. Don't gloss over wrong (25:26). But remember, as we noted in the last chapter, to pay special attention to the timing and tact of your words (see 15:4). The truth can hurt. And we can either wield it carelessly as a blunt instrument to wound, or we can use it skillfully as a surgeon's scalpel to heal.

Genuine Interest and Love

Last, each time we apply the previous seven traits to our counseling, the fragrance of genuine interest and love will linger long in the memory of the one counseled.

Oil and perfume make the heart glad,
So a man's counsel is sweet to his friend. (27:9)

Jonathan's counsel was sweet to David during a very bitter time in his life (see 1 Sam. 19–20; 23:15–18). Paul's counsel surely made Timothy's heart glad when he felt weak and afraid (1 Tim. 4:11–16; 2 Tim. 1:1–14). Why? Was it simply because of the truth David and Timothy received? No, it was because that truth was communicated by close friends whom they knew loved them deeply.

Now that we've examined these eight qualities that make a counselor effective, one question still remains.

Is Counseling Always Successful?

Can any counselor, no matter how well he or she exemplifies tact, objectivity, understanding, and the rest, guarantee the outcome of their advice? Absolutely not. Because even at our best, we are still human and make mistakes. A missed clue or wrong conclusion is all that it takes. Then, too, we're not always given enough time to probe for understanding. And in some cases, no amount of counsel will help because the root problem is medical in origin.

But if a counselor could avoid all those problems, would he or she then always be successful? No again, and Proverbs gives us several reasons why.

1. The Counsel Is Ignored

He is on the path of life who heeds instruction,
But he who forsakes reproof goes astray. (10:17)

The results of any counseling situation ultimately rest in the hands of the counselees. They may be given the best advice, but if they choose to disregard it, nothing will change.

2. They Only Want to Talk

A fool does not delight in understanding,
But only in revealing his own mind. (18:2)

Like the fool, many seek counseling not because they desire insight, direction, or reproof, but because they simply enjoy telling others about their woes. As long as you listen, they'll praise you as a wise and loving counselor. Uncover some of their inadequacies, however, and suddenly you'll find yourself written off as an insensitive brute.

3. They Don't Desire to Change

A man of great anger shall bear the penalty,
For if you rescue him, you will only have to do it
    again. (19:19)

Solomon specifically addresses the angry person who finds greater pleasure in venting anger than in curbing it. Desire, the will to change and give up old habits to take on new, must be present before lasting change can occur.

4. Some Cover Up and Defend

When a wise man has a controversy with a
    foolish man,
The foolish man either rages or laughs, and there
    is no rest. (29:9)

When the counseling hits too close to home, some counselees will attempt to back you off with angry outbursts punctuated with pounding fists and threatening words. Others may laugh inappropriately, as if you had just told the world's funniest joke. All to make you think your advice is nonsense and they can't possibly take it seriously.

5. Simply No Response

A slave will not be instructed by words alone;
For though he understands, there will be no
    response. (29:19)

Commentator Derek Kidner sheds some light on this verse: "This apparently sweeping statement (*cf.* 21) is seen, when balanced by others (*e.g.* 17:2), to refer to the slave mentality, unresponsive, irresponsible."[2] As you may recall from our earlier studies, the mentality of the wise is to embrace reproof. The fool, however, hears and understands wisdom's voice, but does not answer her. Why? Perhaps the will to change is not there. Or maybe this individual wants to snub the person bringing the reproof. The possible reasons are too numerous to list. But, the outcome is always the same—no response, no change.

No counselor can control another person's response to ensure success. What we can do when a counseling situation fails is step back and evaluate, "Was there something I did wrong? Did I overlook something?" If you cannot find anything significant, then rest the case with the Lord. Don't wallow in feelings of guilt or discouragement. God has His own timing for causing people to mature. As Paul said in 1 Corinthians 3, "I planted, Apollos watered, but God was causing the growth" (v. 6).

⚡ Living Insights

As you did in the previous lesson, pause for a little self-evaluation. Circle the number that best represents the strength or weakness of the final three traits in your counseling.

Understanding

1   2   3   4   5   6   7   8   9   10

Honesty

1   2   3   4   5   6   7   8   9   10

Genuine Interest and Love

1   2   3   4   5   6   7   8   9   10

2. Derek Kidner, *The Proverbs: An Introduction and Commentary* (Downers Grove, Ill.: Inter-Varsity Press, 1964), p. 176.

Can you think of a biblical character that best exemplifies each of these traits? How? If not, perhaps you know a godly man or woman who models each of these traits.

Understanding _____

_____

Honesty _____

_____

Genuine Interest and Love _____

_____

☼ *Living Insights* STUDY TWO

Aside from acceptance and a willingness to get involved, what are some other meaningful ways to communicate understanding? For example, body language, the use of questions—think of things that help you know when you're understood.

_____

_____

_____

_____

———————◆———————

Proverbs 29:11 states, "A fool gives full vent to his anger" (NIV). Some people call that being honest. But, as Jay Adams points out in his book *Competent to Counsel,*

> The idea of allowing anger to break out in an un-
> disciplined manner by saying or doing whatever
> comes into mind without weighing the conse-
> quences, without counting ten, without holding it
> back and quieting it, without hearing the whole
> story, is totally wrong. . . . Ventilating sinful feel-
> ings is simply unbiblical. The words "full vent" . . .

mean literally "to send forth all of one's spirit."[3]

Do you sometimes send forth all of your spirit in the name of honesty? Do the people you counsel come away feeling built up and encouraged or bloodied and humiliated? Give a word picture that best describes how you speak the truth in counseling situations.

_____

_____

_____

_____

_____

———————◆———————

"Susan and I have been fighting a lot lately."
"Oh? What's the problem?"
"Money. We can't seem to agree on . . ."
"Have you ever read Larry Burkett's or Ron Blue's books on finances? I tell ya, you and Susan just need to work through some of their books together, and your problems would be over."
"Really?"
"Yeah, great stuff. Since I started following their advice, me and Vicky never fight over finances. You guys will be the same. You'll do fine. Besides, at least you're not in Wilson's shoes. Talk about problems. He went chapter 11 last week and Charlene left him. Well, listen, I gotta run. Get those books. I'll be praying for you."

Look carefully at this casual moment of counseling between two friends, and note all the ways genuine interest and love was or was not communicated. For every negative example you find, give a positive solution.

Negative Example	Positive Solution
_____	_____
_____	_____
_____	_____
_____	_____

3. Jay E. Adams, *Competent to Counsel* (Phillipsburg, N.J.: Presbyterian and Reformed Publishing Co., 1972), p. 221.

Chapter 11

A WOMAN
WORTHY OF PRAISE

Proverbs 31

Among the eloquent sayings of Scripture is a most outstanding treatise on the mother's role. It is both profound and practical . . . full of wise counsel and strong encouragement. Anyone who reads this section realizes that God believes in the woman who gives her home the priority it deserves. He also sees her as a person, distinct and different from her husband, who finds fulfillment in her varied responsibilities and roles.

Right away you sense God's affirming respect as the writer introduces this woman as "an excellent wife."[1]

The eloquent passage, of course, is found in Proverbs 31.

An excellent wife, who can find? (v. 10a)

The Hebrew term used for "excellent" literally means "strength." The New International Version renders this same verse, "A wife of noble character, who can find?" As the question implies, such a woman is rare—and priceless too! "For her worth is far above jewels," the author concludes (v. 10b). Let's hold this precious gem up to the light and note the different facets that make her a woman worthy of praise.

She Has Greatness of Character

Whether she's married or not, at least four qualities define the unmistakable cut of this woman's character.

This message was not a part of the original series but is compatible with it.

1. Charles R. Swindoll, *Living Beyond the Daily Grind (Book II)* (Dallas, Tex.: Word Publishing, 1988), p. 474.

Diligence and a Good Attitude

> She looks for wool and flax,
> And works with her hands in delight. . . .
> She girds herself with strength,
> And makes her arms strong.
> She senses that her gain is good. (vv. 13, 17–18a)

Diligence is more than just using sheer physical energy to finish a task. It is a determination of the will, a commitment to stay at something until it is done and done right. Not only does the praiseworthy woman possess this diligent quality, she adds grace and good humor to it with a delightful attitude.

Industry and Efficiency

> She is like merchant ships;
> She brings her food from afar. . . .
> She considers a field and buys it;
> From her earnings she plants a vineyard. . . .
> She makes linen garments and sells them,
> And supplies belts to the tradesmen.
> (vv. 14, 16, 24)

So much is reflected about this woman's character in these few verses that it's almost blinding. She's a shrewd buyer and seller. She brings home a rich variety of foods for her family. She's a wise investor. "She treats her advantages not as a means to self-indulgence but as a widening of her responsibilities."[2] She's productive, thrifty, always seeking a good return for her labors.

Compassion

> She extends her hand to the poor;
> And she stretches out her hands to the needy. . . .
> She opens her mouth in wisdom,
> And the teaching of kindness is on her tongue.
> (vv. 20, 26)

Many diligent and industrious individuals become too busy, too full of their own self-importance to care about the needs of others.

---

2. Derek Kidner, *The Proverbs: An Introduction and Commentary*, The Tyndale Old Testament Commentaries series (Downers Grove, Ill.: InterVarsity Press, 1964), p. 183.

But not this woman. On the contrary, she reaches out to the home-less, the sick, and the outcast. It is her hand that feeds and her words that comfort.

Beauty Within and Without

> She makes coverings for herself;
> Her clothing is fine linen and purple. . . .
> Strength and dignity are her clothing,
> And she smiles at the future. (vv. 22, 25)

Christians have long fought a tug-of-war with the world over this issue of beauty and where the emphasis should be. Christians pull almost exclusively for inner beauty while the world pulls for dressing up the outer. The woman of praise in Proverbs 31 accom-plishes both. She dresses tastefully, yes, even attractively, on the outside as well as the inside. She possesses beauty of attire and attitude, outer poise and inner personality.

She Is a Devoted Wife

Next, let's set the woman of praise against the background of marriage and see what admirable qualities this highlights.

First, *she maintains her husband's confidence*.

> The heart of her husband trusts in her. (v. 11a)

"Because of her godly character, her husband trusts in her. He has confidence in her, believes in her, and values her judgment."[3] He can be transparent with her, not having to hide his hopes and disappointments, strengths or weaknesses.

Second, *she meets her husband's needs*.

> He will have no lack of gain. (v. 11b)

The praiseworthy wife supports and encourages her husband. She believes in him and builds him up. Rather than using his vulnerabilities against him, she approaches them with sensitivity and gently helps him grow.

Third, *she seeks her husband's good*.

---

3. From the study guide *Building Blocks of Biblical Character*, coauthored by Bryce Klabunde, from the Bible-teaching ministry of Charles R. Swindoll (Anaheim, Calif.: Insight for Living, 1993), p. 66.

She does him good and not evil
All the days of her life. (v. 12)

"Some wives do evil to their husbands," one author observes,

> by needling them with critical remarks or manipu-
> lating them to get their way. History's first wife, Eve,
> gave Adam the fruit forbidden by God; Solomon's
> idol-worshiping wives stole his heart away from God;
> and the woman who symbolizes feminine treachery,
> Jezebel, assisted Ahab in all kinds of evil.[4]

Some wives do good to their husbands by anticipating their
needs, through unexpected acts of kindness, or with unwavering
confidence and respect in good as well as bad times.

Fourth, *she enhances her husband's influence.*

> Her husband is known in the gates,
> When he sits among the elders of the land. (v. 23)

A wife's character and conduct can either strengthen her husband's reputation or weaken it. She may help him earn the respect
of others by her godliness, or she may cause him to lose it through
her folly.

She Is a Dependable Mother

The last backdrop for the woman worthy of praise is motherhood.
And here again we see the glint of several commendable traits.

Disciplined

> She rises also while it is still night,
> And gives food to her household,
> And portions to her maidens. . . .
> Her lamp does not go out at night.
> She stretches out her hands to the distaff,
> And her hands grasp the spindle.
> (vv. 15, 18b–19)

Ask any tired mom—this is an incredibly disciplined woman.
She has the self-control to push herself out of bed before dawn and
prepare breakfast each morning. And this is without the aid of a

4. Swindoll and Klabunde, *Building Blocks,* p. 66.

microwave or Pop-Tarts, mind you. Then she gives out prescribed tasks to her servants, which she probably planned the night before—"her lamp does not go out" (v. 18b). Add to this the fact that she sews regularly to provide for her family, and you can see that she takes the responsibility of running a household seriously.

Organized

> She is not afraid of the snow for her household,
> For all her household are clothed with scarlet. . . .
> She smiles at the future. (vv. 21, 25b)

Commentator Sid Buzzell translates Proverbs' imagery for us:

> Cold weather does not cause this woman to panic for her household . . . ; she is prepared for it. She has clothed them in scarlet, that is, she has provided expensive garments. She spares no cost in protecting her family from the cold.[5]

Dedicated

> She looks well to the ways of her household,
> And does not eat the bread of idleness. (v. 27)

The mark of a dedicated mother is unselfishness. She works constantly to meet the needs of her family, finding time for rest and restoration but not wasting time.

She Is Highly Praised

What are some of the tangible rewards for a life of devotion and dependability?

> Her children bless her (v. 28a).
> Her husband praises her (v. 28b).
> Her peers are challenged by her (v. 29).
> Her works bring her recognition and
> respect (v. 31).
> The Lord is honored by her and
> honors her in return (v. 30).

---

5. Sid S. Buzzell, "Proverbs," in *The Bible Knowledge Commentary*, Old Testament edition, ed. John F. Walvoord and Roy B. Zuck (Wheaton, Ill.: Scripture Press Publications, Victor Books, 1985), p. 973.

Now, as a wife and mother, you're probably saying, "My kids only rise up and bless me when they want something; and if my husband said, 'Many daughters have done nobly, but you excel them all,' to me, I'd probably wonder if he was feeling all right!"

Before you push aside the Proverbs 31 woman as being unrealistic, think about the ways you really do resemble her. Because of you, your family probably eats well, right? They have clothes to wear and a comfortable home to live in. You're probably good at finding bargains. Your children learn valuable lessons about life from you. So don't underestimate yourself! Your family needs you to touch them, to hold them, to give them worth and purpose, dignity and discipline . . . and best of all, your love.[6]

Living Insights

Hello, ladies. I can tell by the look on some of your faces that you're a little queasy about tackling this Living Insight. You're thinking, "He's probably going to ask me to compare myself to Wonder Woman in Proverbs 31 and note all my weaknesses. Great. Just what I need—more guilt."

Nope. I'm not going to do that. In fact, I'd like you to do just the opposite. I want you to give me at least one *positive* example from your life of each trait listed in the lesson. Why? Because often all we see are the negatives, the mistakes, the shortcomings, without giving our good works their proper due. I want you to be encouraged, not discouraged. You do far more than you probably give yourself credit for. So, as we said in the lesson, don't underestimate yourself!

Now go to it. Take a fun and affirming look at the good in yourself—you've earned it.

Married or Unmarried

Diligence and a Good Attitude _____

_____

Industry and Efficiency _____

_____

6. Adapted from Swindoll and Klabunde, *Building Blocks*, pp. 68–69.

Compassion _____

_____

Beauty Within and Without _____

_____

Married

Maintain My Husband's Confidence _____

_____

Meet My Husband's Needs _____

_____

Seek My Husband's Good _____

_____

Enhance My Husband's Influence _____

_____

Mother

Disciplined _____

_____

Organized _____

_____

Dedicated _____

_____

Living Insights

Hello, husbands. Now it's your turn. This is your chance to do just as Proverbs 31:28–29 suggests—praise your wives. Identify at least one specific way your wife models the qualities of a woman worthy of praise. Then do that—praise her. Get the kids involved in helping you do this as well, and water the good that this mother and wife does with kind words of affirmation and appreciation.

Diligence and a Good Attitude _____

_____

Industry and Efficiency _____

_____

Compassion _____

_____

Beauty Within and Without _____

_____

Maintains Her Husband's Confidence _____

_____

Meets Her Husband's Needs _____

_____

Seeks Her Husband's Good _____

_____

Enhances Her Husband's Influence _____

_____

Disciplined _____

_____

Organized _____

_____

Dedicated _____

_____

Chapter 12

TURNING KNOWLEDGE INTO WISDOM

Proverbs 1:1–2:6

As Haddon Robinson reminded us at the start of our study, "Knowledge is not enough to meet life's problems. We need wisdom, the ability to handle life with skill."[1] He's right, of course, and we've gleaned many wonderful pearls for doing just that— living wisely—in our study together of Proverbs. But now the time has come for us to pursue wisdom down our own separate paths. As a final farewell, take with you these five reminders for turning knowledge into wisdom.

First, *read Proverbs regularly*. Remember Solomon's purposes for writing?

> To know wisdom and instruction,
> To discern the sayings of understanding,
> To receive instruction in wise behavior,
> Righteousness, justice and equity;
> To give prudence to the naive,
> To the youth knowledge and discretion,
> A wise man will hear and increase in learning,
> And a man of understanding will acquire wise
>   counsel,
> To understand a proverb and a figure,
> The words of the wise and their riddles. (1:2–6)

Are you that man or woman of understanding who wants to acquire wise counsel? Then continue mining Proverbs. Dig a little deeper each day. Meditate on what you read. Memorize as much as you can, and apply it everywhere you can.

Second, *hear and heed your parents' counsel*. Proverbs is not the only fountain of wisdom. From the mouths of godly moms and dads flow much-needed practical insights and guidance.

This message was not a part of the original series but is compatible with it.

1. Haddon Robinson, from the foreword to Robert L. Alden's *Proverbs: A Commentary on an Ancient Book of Timeless Advice* (Grand Rapids, Mich.: Baker Book House, 1983), p. 7.

Hear, my son, your father's instruction,
And do not forsake your mother's teaching;
Indeed, they are a graceful wreath to your head,
And ornaments about your neck. (vv. 8–9)

No one knows you better than your parents. No one believes in you more than they do. And no one will stay by your side longer than they will. Listen to their advice. Accept their counsel with humility and gratefulness. That's not to say you must always agree with them or always do as they suggest, especially when you're a mature adult. But hear them out with the respect they deserve as your God-given guardians.

Third, *choose your friends carefully*. Albert Schweitzer once said, "Example is not the main thing in influencing others. It is the only thing."[2] How are you being influenced by your friends' example? For good? Do they bring out the best in you? Or do you need to avoid some of them, as Solomon warns?

If sinners entice you,
Do not consent.
If they say, "Come with us,
Let us lie in wait for blood,
Let us ambush the innocent without cause;
Let us swallow them alive like Sheol,
Even whole, as those who go down to the pit;
We shall find all kinds of precious wealth,
We shall fill our houses with spoil;
Throw in your lot with us,
We shall all have one purse,"
My son, do not walk in the way with them.
Keep your feet from their path,
For their feet run to evil,
And they hasten to shed blood. . . .
But they lie in wait for their own blood;
They ambush their own lives. (vv. 10–16, 18)

Notice what this passage points out about foolish friends:

- They do harm to others (v. 11).

2. Albert Schweitzer, as quoted in *Quotable Quotations*, comp. Lloyd Cory (Wheaton, Ill.: Scripture Press Publications, Victor Books, 1985), p. 120.

- They make promises they can't keep (v. 13).

- They want you to join them—not the other way around (v. 14).

- They are attracted to the wrong activities (v. 16).

- They hurt themselves (v. 18).

If you're just now entering that phase of life when your friends have more of your attention and time than your parents, choose your companions carefully . . . you're choosing your character (see 1 Cor. 15:33).

Fourth, *pay attention to life's reproofs.* You remember this. We devoted an entire chapter to the importance of heeding Lady Wisdom (see "Warnings against Refusing Reproof").

> Wisdom shouts in the street,
> She lifts her voice in the square;
> At the head of the noisy streets she cries out;
> At the entrance of the gates in the city, she
> utters her sayings:
> "How long, O naive ones, will you love simplicity?
> And scoffers delight themselves in scoffing,
> And fools hate knowledge?
> Turn to my reproof,
> Behold, I will pour out my spirit on you;
> I will make my words known to you." (vv. 20–23)

It's no great tragedy when any of us makes a mistake. That's natural. That's human. The tragedy comes, however, when we fail to learn from those mistakes. Like the naive, the scoffer, and the fool, some people just keep making the same senseless mistakes over and over, foolishly ignoring wisdom's admonitions. Before they know it, they lose their sense of right and wrong, their character, friends, businesses, and joy. Then they wonder why life isn't working for them.

Wisdom says, "Break away! Come to your senses and heed my voice. Follow me to the path of wisdom and righteousness. Regain your life."

Fifth, *pray that you will gain wisdom as you grow.* In his usual forthright way, the apostle James wrote, "If any of you lacks wisdom, let him ask of God, who gives to all men generously and without reproach, and it will be given to him" (James 1:5). Solomon echoes this same advice with his usual eloquence.

If you will receive my sayings,
And treasure my commandments within you,
Make your ear attentive to wisdom,
Incline your heart to understanding;
For if you cry for discernment,
Lift your voice for understanding;
If you seek her as silver,
And search for her as for hidden treasures;
Then you will discern the fear of the Lord,
And discover the knowledge of God.
For the Lord gives wisdom;
From His mouth come knowledge and understanding.
He stores up sound wisdom for the upright;
He is a shield to those who walk in integrity,
Guarding the paths of justice,
And He preserves the way of His godly ones.
Then you will discern righteousness and justice
And equity and every good course.
For wisdom will enter your heart,
And knowledge will be pleasant to your soul.
(Prov. 2:1–10)

I read hard work here, don't you? Note the miner's terms and imagery Solomon employs. He wants us to dig with our voices, labor diligently in our supplications—asking, searching for God's precious gems of wisdom.

Do more, however, than just jackhammer the Lord with requests. Pause to listen. Slow down and meditatively consider your need before the Lord. Be still and allow His Spirit to minister to you.

There you are, my friend. Take these five jewels of wisdom on your journey, and they will lead you to even greater riches of understanding, instruction, righteousness, prudence, and discretion. King Solomon's treasures will be yours, making you a very wealthy person in the skill of wise living.

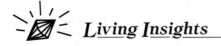 **Living Insights** STUDY ONE

Have you "ambushed" your own life by the friends you've chosen to be your closest companions (1:18)? Let's think about that for a moment.

❑ Do they intentionally harm others, verbally or physically? Are they revengeful and mean?

❑ Do they make commitments they can't keep? Have they disappointed and hurt you more than once with broken promises?

❑ Are you always having to bend to their wishes? Is it a one-sided relationship that ignores your desires and needs?

❑ Must you violate your conscience in order to participate in some of the things they do?

❑ Would you say that your friends' lifestyles today are preparing them for wise living in the future? Or are they making choices and behaving in ways that are leading toward heartache?

Perhaps none of this is true of your best friends, and that's great. In that case, shift your focus to the positive ways they model wisdom.

What is it that you like about them? How do they exemplify understanding? Do they model discernment? In what ways have you seen them handle life with skill?

_____

_____

_____

_____

_____

_____

_____

_____

Last, let your buddies or girlfriends know what you appreciate about them. Tell them you've been learning about wise living from Proverbs and that you've seen them model it for you in some specific ways that you want to affirm.

And if they're *not* "good" friends?

> My son, do not walk in the way with them.
> Keep your feet from their path. (1:15)

 *Living Insights*

It's time to collect all the jewels you've unearthed from our study of Proverbs. Use the space provided to go back and note the one or two most significant insights you dug up in each chapter.

Vertical Wisdom for Horizontal Living _____

_____

_____

Warnings against Refusing Reproof _____

_____

_____

For Miners Only _____

_____

_____

You and Your Heart _____

_____

_____

You and Your Tongue _____

_____

_____

The Poison in Your Mouth _____

_____

_____

You and Your Job (Part One) _____

_____

_____

You and Your Job (Part Two) _____

_____

_____

You and Your Counseling (Part One) _____

_____

_____

You and Your Counseling (Part Two) _____

_____

_____

A Woman Worthy of Praise _____

_____

_____

Turning Knowledge into Wisdom _____

_____

_____

BOOKS FOR PROBING FURTHER

God's wise words to us through His servant Solomon have indeed been "better than the profit of silver" and "more precious than jewels" (Prov. 3:14a, 15a). As you continue mining the wealth of Proverbs and digging deeper into the topics of our study, we hope some of the following books will help make your efforts more precise and enriching.

The Book of Proverbs

Alden, Robert L. *Proverbs: A Commentary on an Ancient Book of Timeless Advice*. Grand Rapids, Mich.: Baker Book House, 1983.

Kidner, Derek. *The Proverbs: An Introduction and Commentary*. Tyndale Old Testament Commentaries series. Downers Grove, Ill.: InterVarsity Press, 1964.

Pursuing Wisdom

Bonhoeffer, Dietrich. *Meditating on the Word*. Translated and edited by David McI. Gracie. Cambridge, Mass.: Cowley Publications, 1986.

You and Your Tongue

Mains, Karen Burton. *You Are What You Say: Cure for the Troublesome Tongue*. Grand Rapids, Mich.: Zondervan Publishing House, 1988.

Mayhall, Carole. *Words That Hurt, Words That Heal*. Colorado Springs, Colo.: NavPress, 1986.

Virkler, Henry A. *Speaking Your Mind without Stepping on Toes*. Wheaton, Ill.: Scripture Press Publications, Victor Books, 1991.

You and Your Job

Briles, Judith, Luci Swindoll, and Mary Whelchel. *The Workplace: Questions Women Ask*. Today's Christian Woman Series. Carol Stream, Ill.: Christianity Today; Portland, Oreg.: Multnomah Press, 1992.

Campolo, Tony. *Everything You've Heard Is Wrong*. Dallas, Tex.: Word Publishing, 1992.

Sherman, Doug, and William Hendricks. *Your Work Matters to God*. Colorado Springs, Colo.: NavPress, 1987.

Swindoll, Luci. *After You've Dressed for Success: A Guide to Developing Character as Well as a Career*. Waco, Tex.: Word Books, Publisher, 1987.

You and Your Counseling

Biebel, David B. *How to Help a Heartbroken Friend*. Nashville, Tenn.: Thomas Nelson Publishers, 1993.

Buchanan, Duncan. *The Counselling of Jesus*. The Jesus Library series. Downers Grove, Ill.: InterVarsity Press, 1985.

Crabb, Lawrence J., Jr. *Basic Principles of Biblical Counseling*. Grand Rapids, Mich.: Zondervan Publishing House, Ministry Resources Library, 1975.

————. *Effective Biblical Counseling*. Grand Rapids, Mich.: Zondervan Publishing House, Ministry Resources Library, 1977.

————. *Understanding People*. Grand Rapids, Mich.: Zondervan Publishing House, Ministry Resources Library, 1987.

D'Arcy, Paula. *When Your Friend Is Grieving: Building a Bridge of Love*. Wheaton, Ill.: Harold Shaw Publishers, 1990.

Swindoll, Charles R. *Encourage Me*. Portland, Oreg.: Multnomah Press, 1982.

Some of the books listed above may be out of print and available only through a library. For those currently available, please contact your local Christian bookstore. Books by Charles R. Swindoll are available through Insight for Living. IFL also offers some books by other authors—please note the ordering information that follows and contact the office that serves you.

NOTES

NOTES

NOTES

NOTES

NOTES

NOTES

ORDERING INFORMATION

SELECTED STUDIES FROM PROVERBS

Cassette Tapes and Study Guide

This Bible study guide was designed to be used independently or in conjunction with the broadcast of Chuck Swindoll's taped messages which are listed below. If you would like to order cassette tapes or further copies of this study guide, please see the information given below and the order form provided at the end of this guide.

		U.S.	Canada
PRO SG	Study guide	$ 3.95	$ 5.25
PRO CS	Cassette series, includes album cover	42.55	51.25
PRO 1–6	Individual cassettes, includes messages A and B	ea. 6.30	ea. 8.00

The prices are subject to change without notice.

PRO 1-A: *Vertical Wisdom for Horizontal Living*—Proverbs 1:1–9
B: *Warnings against Refusing Reproof*— Proverbs 1:20–33

PRO 2-A: *For Miners Only*—Proverbs 2:1–9
B: *You and Your Heart*—Selected Proverbs

PRO 3-A: *You and Your Tongue*—Selected Proverbs
B: *The Poison in Your Mouth*—Selected Proverbs

PRO 4-A: *You and Your Job (Part One)*—Selected Proverbs
B: *You and Your Job (Part Two)*—Selected Proverbs

PRO 5-A: *You and Your Counseling (Part One)*—Selected Proverbs
B: *You and Your Counseling (Part Two)*—Selected Proverbs

PRO 6-A: *A Woman Worthy of Praise**— Proverbs 31
B: *Turning Knowledge into Wisdom**—Proverbs 1:1–2:6

*These messages were not a part of the original series but are compatible with it.

How to Order by Phone or FAX
(Credit card orders only)

United States: 1-800-772-8888 from 7:00 A.M. to 4:30 P.M., Pacific time, Monday through Friday
FAX (714) 575-5496 anytime, day or night

Canada: 1-800-663-7639, Vancouver residents call (604) 596-2910 from 7:00 A.M. to 5:00 P.M., Pacific time, Monday through Friday
FAX (604) 596-2975 anytime, day or night

Australia: (03) 872-4606 or FAX (03) 874-8890 from 9:00 A.M. to 5:00 P.M., Monday through Friday

---

Other International Locations: call the Ordering Services Department in the United States at (714) 575-5000 during the hours listed above.

How to Order by Mail

United States
- Mail to: Ordering Services Department
  Insight for Living
  Post Office Box 69000
  Anaheim, CA 92817-0900
- Sales tax: California residents add 7.25%.
- Shipping: add 10% of the total order amount for first-class delivery. (Otherwise, allow four to six weeks for fourth-class delivery.)
- Payment: personal checks, money orders, credit cards (Visa, MasterCard, Discover Card, and American Express). No invoices or COD orders available.
- $10 fee for *any* returned check.

Canada
- Mail to: Insight for Living Ministries
  Post Office Box 2510
  Vancouver, BC V6B 3W7
- Sales tax: please add 7% GST. British Columbia residents also add 7% sales tax (on tapes or cassette series).
- Shipping: included in prices listed above.
- Payment: personal checks, money orders, credit cards (Visa, Master-Card). No invoices or COD orders available.

- Delivery: approximately four weeks.

Australia, New Zealand, or Papua New Guinea
- Mail to: Insight for Living, Inc.
  GPO Box 2823 EE
  Melbourne, Victoria 3001, Australia
- Shipping and delivery time: please see chart that follows.
- Payment: personal checks payable in U.S. funds, international money orders, or credit cards (Visa, MasterCard).

Other International Locations
- Mail to: Ordering Services Department
  Insight for Living
  Post Office Box 69000
  Anaheim, CA 92817-0900
- Shipping and delivery time: please see chart that follows.
- Payment: personal checks payable in U.S. funds, international money orders, or credit cards (Visa, MasterCard, and American Express).

Type of Shipping	Postage Cost	Delivery
Surface	10% of total order*	6 to 10 weeks
Airmail	25% of total order*	under 6 weeks

*Use U.S. price as a base.

Our Guarantee
Your complete satisfaction is our top priority here at Insight for Living. If you're not completely satisfied with anything you order, please return it for full credit, a refund, or a replacement, as *you* prefer.

Insight for Living Catalog
The Insight for Living catalog features study guides, tapes, and books by a variety of Christian authors. To obtain a free copy, call us at the numbers listed above.

Order Form
United States, Australia, and Other International Locations
(Canadian residents please use order form on reverse side.)

PRO CS represents the entire *Selected Studies from Proverbs* series in a special album cover, while PRO 1–6 are the individual tapes included in the series. PRO SG represents this study guide, should you desire to order additional copies.

PRO	SG	Study guide	$ 3.95
PRO	CS	Cassette series, includes album cover	42.55
PRO	1–6	Individual cassettes, includes messages A and B	ea. 6.30

Product Code	Product Description	Quantity	Unit Price	Total
			$	$
		Subtotal		
	California Residents—Sales Tax *Add 7.25% of subtotal.*			
	U.S. First-Class Shipping *For faster delivery, add 10% for postage and handling.*			
	Non-United States Residents *U.S. price plus 10% surface postage or 25% airmail.*			
	Gift to Insight for Living *Tax-deductible in the United States.*			
	Total Amount Due *Please do not send cash.*		$	

Prices are subject to change without notice.

Payment by: ❏ Check or money order payable to Insight for Living   ❏ Credit card

(Circle one):   Visa   MasterCard   Discover Card   American Express

Number _____

Expiration Date _____   Signature _____
We cannot process your credit card purchase without your signature.

Name _____

Address _____

City _____   State _____

Zip Code _____   Country _____

Telephone (_____) _____   Radio Station ____ ____ ____ ____
If questions arise concerning your order, we may need to contact you.

Mail this order form to the Ordering Services Department at one of these addresses:

Insight for Living
Post Office Box 69000, Anaheim, CA 92817-0900

Insight for Living, Inc.
GPO Box 2823 EE, Melbourne, VIC 3001, Australia

Order Form
Canadian Residents

(Residents of the United States, Australia, and other international locations, please use order form on reverse side.)

PRO CS represents the entire *Selected Studies from Proverbs* series in a special album cover, while PRO 1–6 are the individual tapes included in the series. PRO SG represents this study guide, should you desire to order additional copies.

PRO	SG	Study guide	$ 5.25
PRO	CS	Cassette series, includes album cover	51.25
PRO	1–6	Individual cassettes, includes messages A and B	ea. 8.00

Product Code	Product Description	Quantity	Unit Price	Total
			$	$
		Subtotal		
		Add 7% GST		
		British Columbia Residents *Add 7% sales tax on individual tapes or cassette series.*		
		Gift to Insight for Living Ministries *Tax-deductible in Canada.*		
		Total Amount Due *Please do not send cash.*	$	

Prices are subject to change without notice.

Payment by: ❑ Check or money order payable to Insight for Living Ministries
❑ Credit card

(Circle one): Visa   MasterCard   Number _____

Expiration Date _____ Signature _____
<small>We cannot process your credit card purchase without your signature.</small>

Name _____

Address _____

City _____ Province _____

Postal Code _____ Country _____

Telephone (___) _____ Radio Station ____ ____ ____ ____
If questions arise concerning your order, we may need to contact you.

Mail this order form to the Ordering Services Department at the following address:

Insight for Living Ministries
Post Office Box 2510
Vancouver, BC, Canada V6B 3W7

Order Form
United States, Australia, and Other International Locations
(Canadian residents please use order form on reverse side.)

PRO CS represents the entire *Selected Studies from Proverbs* series in a special album cover, while PRO 1–6 are the individual tapes included in the series. PRO SG represents this study guide, should you desire to order additional copies.

PRO	SG	Study guide	$ 3.95
PRO	CS	Cassette series, includes album cover	42.55
PRO	1–6	Individual cassettes, includes messages A and B	ea. 6.30

Product Code	Product Description	Quantity	Unit Price	Total
			$	$
		Subtotal		
	California Residents—Sales Tax Add 7.25% of subtotal.			
	U.S. First-Class Shipping For faster delivery, add 10% for postage and handling.			
	Non-United States Residents U.S. price plus 10% surface postage or 25% airmail.			
	Gift to Insight for Living Tax-deductible in the United States.			
	Total Amount Due Please do not send cash.		$	

Prices are subject to change without notice.

Payment by: ❑ Check or money order payable to Insight for Living ❑ Credit card

(Circle one): Visa MasterCard Discover Card American Express

Number_____

Expiration Date_____ Signature_____
<small>We cannot process your credit card purchase without your signature.</small>

Name_____

Address_____

City_____ State_____

Zip Code_____ Country_____

Telephone (_____)_____ Radio Station____ ____ ____ ____
If questions arise concerning your order, we may need to contact you.

Mail this order form to the Ordering Services Department at one of these addresses:

Insight for Living
Post Office Box 69000, Anaheim, CA 92817-0900

Insight for Living, Inc.
GPO Box 2823 EE, Melbourne, VIC 3001, Australia

Order Form
Canadian Residents
(Residents of the United States, Australia, and other international locations, please use order form on reverse side.)

PRO CS represents the entire *Selected Studies from Proverbs* series in a special album cover, while PRO 1–6 are the individual tapes included in the series. PRO SG represents this study guide, should you desire to order additional copies.

PRO	SG	Study guide	$ 5.25
PRO	CS	Cassette series, includes album cover	51.25
PRO	1–6	Individual cassettes, includes messages A and B	ea. 8.00

Product Code	Product Description	Quantity	Unit Price	Total
			$	$
		Subtotal		
		Add 7% GST		
		British Columbia Residents *Add 7% sales tax on individual tapes or cassette series.*		
		Gift to Insight for Living Ministries *Tax-deductible in Canada.*		
		Total Amount Due *Please do not send cash.*	$	

Prices are subject to change without notice.

Payment by: ❑ Check or money order payable to Insight for Living Ministries
❑ Credit card

(Circle one): Visa   MasterCard   Number _____

Expiration Date _____   Signature _____
We cannot process your credit card purchase without your signature.

Name _____

Address _____

City _____   Province _____

Postal Code _____   Country _____

Telephone (_____) _____   Radio Station ____ ____ ____ ____
If questions arise concerning your order, we may need to contact you.

Mail this order form to the Ordering Services Department at the following address:

Insight for Living Ministries
Post Office Box 2510
Vancouver, BC, Canada V6B 3W7

CCCC

Order Form
United States, Australia, and Other International Locations
(Canadian residents please use order form on reverse side.)

PRO CS represents the entire *Selected Studies from Proverbs* series in a special album cover, while PRO 1–6 are the individual tapes included in the series. PRO SG represents this study guide, should you desire to order additional copies.

PRO	SG	Study guide	$ 3.95
PRO	CS	Cassette series, includes album cover	42.55
PRO	1–6	Individual cassettes, includes messages A and B	ea. 6.30

Product Code	Product Description	Quantity	Unit Price	Total
			$	$
		Subtotal		
	California Residents—Sales Tax *Add 7.25% of subtotal.*			
	U.S. First-Class Shipping *For faster delivery, add 10% for postage and handling.*			
	Non-United States Residents *U.S. price plus 10% surface postage or 25% airmail.*			
	Gift to Insight for Living *Tax-deductible in the United States.*			
	Total Amount Due *Please do not send cash.*		$	

Prices are subject to change without notice.

Payment by: ❑ Check or money order payable to Insight for Living   ❑ Credit card

(Circle one):   Visa   MasterCard   Discover Card   American Express

Number _____

Expiration Date _____   Signature _____
We cannot process your credit card purchase without your signature.

Name _____

Address _____

City _____   State _____

Zip Code _____   Country _____

Telephone (____) _____   Radio Station ____ ____ ___-____
If questions arise concerning your order, we may need to contact you.

Mail this order form to the Ordering Services Department at one of these addresses:

Insight for Living
Post Office Box 69000, Anaheim, CA 92817-0900

Insight for Living, Inc.
GPO Box 2823 EE, Melbourne, VIC 3001, Australia

Order Form
Canadian Residents
(Residents of the United States, Australia, and other international locations,
please use order form on reverse side.)

PRO CS represents the entire *Selected Studies from Proverbs* series in a special album cover, while PRO 1–6 are the individual tapes included in the series. PRO SG represents this study guide, should you desire to order additional copies.

PRO	SG	Study guide	$ 5.25
PRO	CS	Cassette series, includes album cover	51.25
PRO	1–6	Individual cassettes, includes messages A and B	ea. 8.00

Product Code	Product Description	Quantity	Unit Price	Total
			$	$
		Subtotal		
		Add 7% GST		
		British Columbia Residents *Add 7% sales tax on individual tapes or cassette series.*		
		Gift to Insight for Living Ministries *Tax-deductible in Canada.*		
		Total Amount Due *Please do not send cash.*	$	

Prices are subject to change without notice.

Payment by: ❑ Check or money order payable to Insight for Living Ministries
❑ Credit card

(Circle one): Visa   MasterCard   Number_____

Expiration Date_____   Signature_____
We cannot process your credit card purchase without your signature.

Name_____

Address_____

City_____   Province_____

Postal Code_____   Country_____

Telephone (____)_____   Radio Station____ ____ ____ ____
If questions arise concerning your order, we may need to contact you.

Mail this order form to the Ordering Services Department at the following address:

Insight for Living Ministries
Post Office Box 2510
Vancouver, BC, Canada V6B 3W7